Contents

17th November 2011

ISBN-13: **978-1466360570** (CreateSpace-Assigned)

ISBN-10: **1466360577**

BISAC: **History / Revolutionary**

Introduction

The aim of this short book is to bring together for the first time in the English language a history based on a Marxist interpretation of class relations in Greek society at the turn of the 20th century. How the Greek labour movement was formed, influenced and in turn grew till the outbreak of WWII. Information is provided regarding the groups that constituted the birth of the Greek labour movement and its eventual domination by the Stalinist wing of the Russian labour movement. New information on the rise and growth of the Archeio-Marxist wing of the early years of the growth of Greek communism also becomes available in English for the first time.

Another article gives light to the history of the Macedonian question which divided the Balkan movement in general as well as a section of the debate of the abstentionist wing of the Greek Trotskyist movement in relation to the KKE and the armed partisan resistance against the German occupation.

The aim of course is to provide another angle to the history of the Greek labour movement from a variety of sources so as to enrich an understanding of the past so the mistakes of yesteryear aren't repeated in the struggles of today.

VN Gelis

1st November 2011

The Impact of the Russian Revolution on the Greek Labour Movement

The impact of the Russian Revolution on labour movements throughout Europe was in many ways decisive. Greece was no exception to this process. Basically an agricultural country, a proletariat did emerge and all its important first steps were related in one way or another with the developments in the USSR.

From the founding of GSEE (Greek Trade-Union Federation), through to the struggle for a Communist Party, the nascent Greek proletariat underwent many stages of development as well as crises. The anti-working class nature of all Greek governments in the 1920's meant that the communist movement developed under conditions of illegality and harsh persecutions. But the ideals of the Russian Revolution nevertheless influenced a significant section of the Greek working class. The tragedy is that these ideals in the space of a few years were to be trample upon by the domination of stalinism in the USSR. As in other European Communist Parties resistance to stalinisim ocurred, but it proved unable to reverse the course history had chosen.

**In attempting to find the source material for this analysis it must be taken into account that many original sources no longer exist due to the harsh repressions of the Greek state against the left, as well as the fact that hardly any studies on the history of the Greek labour movement have been made in Greece and only one has ever appeared in English: D. G. Kousoulas, Revolution and Defeat: The Story of the Greek Communist Party.

PART A
The Nature of Greek Society at the Beginning of the 20th Century

The Greek Revolution of 1821 was undoubtedly a bourgeois national revolution. Generally speaking the task of the bourgeois revolution from the previous century was obviously determined from the level of development of the productive forces. The creation of modern nations which presupposed the solution of feudal dues and the aristocracy, in other words the old productive relations which were based on the dependence of the farmer to the aristocrat or the big landowner.

It was a revolution of national independence whose aim was to clarify the national borders, to create a national language, education, religion, and all the other structures which were to be found in other countries such as Italy, France, Germany etc. and above all to create the land which they can form current social classes, the bourgeoisie and the proletariat.

The bourgeois revolution couldn't base a true and clear democracy a true economic and political independence and equality of the nations. This is the task of the socialist revolution which having abolished classes and conflicting classes and national borders will create a new human world.

Thus if the revolution of 1821 didn't manage to create a true independence for the Greek people that doesn't negate its bourgeois character. That which it must note is that the revolution despite being bourgeois, didn't manage to create total bourgeois rule but a bourgeois feudal coalition. It was a revolution which in its results didn't manage to geographically complete the Greek state. 1821 wasn't but the first dose of the bourgeois revolution, which required another century for its eventual conclusion.

There is no need to refer to the obstacles which were placed in front of the bourgeoisie in order to complete its total rule. Only to add that the revolution didn't win totally in particular the battle of the Greeks in Keratsini against the Turks and the death of Karaiskakis.

The declaration of Greek independence was the result of diplomatic manoeuvres amongst the collapsing Ottoman Empire and the three great forces of England, France and Tsarist Russia. These forces wanted Greece as a provisional bulwark against Turkey and for the Greek nation to be mixed especially in Pelloponiso.

But the Greek people fought through a whole series of wars and revolutions and achieved despite the wish of the 'big' dominating powers, their national independent existence. But this was a long and arduous process. Until 1900 the ruling bourgeois faction shared its power with landowners and aristocrats and was unable to fight for its total independence and its absolute right to rule.

The first quarter of the 20th century was a turning point in the right for the bourgeoisie to complete the uncompleted bourgeois democratic rights of the revolution of 1821. Through two revolutions in 1909 and 1922 and through endless Balkan wars, Greece completed its bourgeois transformation.

The Historical Background of the Movement of Bourgeois Transformation

Up until the last decade of the last century, the great mass of people in Greece were farmers. A few cities like Athens, Piraues, Siros, Volos to which the social position of the citizens was unclear. After 1890 with the development of transport, public works and taxation which the Tricoupis government imposed. There was a rapid growth of small businesses and industries. From then a rapid rise occurs of the bourgeoisie which starts to get stronger and the proletariat starts to grow as well. Especially after 1900 and thereafter the rhythm of development becomes more pronounced. In 1892 the total value of industrial production was equivalent to 42 billion drachmas. By 1911-12 the value of investments had risen to 230 billion. But the agricultural basis of the economy was clear. The most backward forms of production existed, the independent farmers and petty businessmen who still hadn't been unified in a national market.

In the administration of the state the 'aristocratic' oligarchy was in majority and the population was under fierce oppression and administrative punitive taxation. The farmers handed over 40% of the taxable earnings of the state whilst the oligarchy was totally untaxed. The indirect taxes on consumable goods ranged from 30-1,400%. Bourgeois and petty-bourgeois under the pressure of the oligarchy became stronger instead of weaker. The necessity to resist to the uneven treatment created a whole layer of educated and ideological leaders.

The same happened with the farmers whose position was more untenable in relation to any other class. The farmers were obliged to give to the landowner boss around one third or even half of their produce, from their cattle sheep, chickens, lambs and other animals as well as butter, wood and even to send a female member of the family to make the bread, a tradition which was equal to that of the landowners right to sleep with the bride on the first night. The landowners had the right to everything and people were not allowed to leave the village without the right of the landowner's spies as well as not having the right to cultivate land in other areas, also to not have the right to own land. The farmers lived in huts and they ate alongside their animals and when the landowner came they had to bow down to him and to bang with their forehead three times the ground and to kiss his left foot. They used to also get whipped publicly if they committed any misdemeanour which the landowner heard about. This situation had enraged the landless farmers especially in Thessalia, who were very receptive to revolutionary calls. They had found themselves their own leaders like S. Triantafillidis who propagated the expropriation of the landowners and the 'socialist' M. Antipas who was murdered by the landowners.

The situation of the farmers and the poor layers inside the cities and villages especially after the defeat of the Greek army in its war with Turkey in 1897. Thessaly which was the northern most part of Greece at the time was evacuated and its people were turned into refugees as a result poverty increased tremendously.

The situation in the Army was analogous. The war had created an anti-western climate of the lower ranks of officers who hated the monarchy, the aristocracy and the old parties as represented by the Theotokis government. The officers believed quite rightly the old ruling classes as being responsible for the disorganisation and the decay which dominated the country as a result of the denigrating defeat of 1897. The organisation of the soldiers was disastrous. In reality it was just groups of armed men scattered all over the country with old and broker from the war weaponry. There were only 12,000 men who were responsible of carrying out police tasks for more criminals in the country. These criminal gangs had been created and had flooded Greece after the war mostly made up of demobilised soldiers or escapees from the army.

This problem the Theotokis government was able to solve by pretending it didn't notice the exodus of thousands of these brigand gangs to North America. Many of these murderers and animal thieves managed to enrich themselves in America and they returned to Greece opening up businesses. Such are some of the roots of the modern bourgeoisie in Greece.

During the same period the Ottoman Empire is being convulsed by an internal revolutionary wave of the Neo-Turks whose declarations influenced many Greek officers who started to copy them. Inside the barracks many conflicts broke out as the younger officers spoke openly about politics and they criticised their 'superiors'. The officers who were basically men from poor backgrounds created their own Union. They were the most ripped off section. They are the ones who did all the work training the young soldiers, whilst the big chiefs, the 'red socked' (nickname given to them because of the colour of their socks) never even went to their barracks.

Amongst the officers who had broader aspirations was Nikolaos Plastiras and George Kondilis. The Union of Officers had secret meetings with bourgeois oppositionists, lawyers, journalists, sociologists men who were later supporters of Venizelism (led by Venizelos).

In the army as well as in the popular masses the slogan "Resurrection" which was first heard from the newspaper 'Acropolis' (publisher was G. Gabrilidis) became the most popular. The lower rank of officers embedded with national traditions, proposing above all the national issues was from the beginning of this century as in 1843 and in 1862 the vanguard of this movements, as the bourgeoisie was condemned into a historical weakness, unable to take the lead and defeat the old order and impose its own.

Apart from all the other problems Theotokis' government had other issues to confront such as the Cretan one, which became a point of betrayal and denigration of the Greek peoples by the big 'defending' powers.

Venizelos had decisively and in an armed fashion agreed to declare a union of the large island with Greece. He had organised guerrilla detachments in Therisso. But the oligarchic aristocracy which ruled Greece didn't have the will to go against the wishes of the Anglo-French and Russians.

These 'protectors' of Greece gave to the Foreign Minister Baldatzi a declaration in which the 'high level rights' of the Sultan of Crete are guaranteed. The Theotokis government weathered the attack without muttering a word. The essence of the declaration and the problematic tone with which it was formulated made led to hatred for the people and the army everywhere in the houses, in the shops, in the cafes, in the streets and everywhere we had big discussions disputes and very bad words for Theotokis and the Palace. From the moment Venizelos movement arose in Crete the propaganda machine from the old order towards the people was a clear line in opposition against the big powers and union would be achieved. But the declarations from those big powers froze all and weakened the honour of the people making all go mad against the foreign 'defenders' and their local lackeys.

The Insurrection in the Peloponnese

After the defeat of 1897 many officers were demobilised and many incensed and disgusted were defeated. Many of these didn't hide their reactionary ideas and openly condemned George 1st.

A true republican, Fikoris who had been given medals in honour for his service in the war returned to his place of residence, Sparta, and started openly propaganda against the monarchy. Fikioris found and organised other followers and in 1900 declared an insurrection. "The fact that our rulers are treading on everything human and holy is well known to many… But the people have the right according to the article 110 of the Constitution to defend their rights… we are in the mountains - wrote Fikioris in his declaration - to hunt down the tax collectors who have sucked clean our blood and turned us into beggars due to the disastrous and traitorous war of 1897 which has turned us into slaves of foreign powers. It is a disgrace to accept these brigand rulers, who two years after the betrayal are at it again. Now it is a disgrace for Greek people and foreigners to condemn us that we are not the children of our forefathers. We are not demanding our rights and if the deserters (he is referring to the general staff of 97) was for strangling we are all for strangling as we didn't strangle them. Forward then men, the nation is ill, God blesses, the law is rotten, your honour is at stake, poverty threatens you. The undefeated Deleris with the sword in had screams at you.

"Men if you want freedom and a nation, stand tall and follow me, find traitors and kill them."
J. Fikioris Ex-Officer

The government sent an army against Fikioris and forced him to retreat into mount Taijetos. There they circled him and killed him after heroic resistance. As can be seen from his declaration he wasn't but a radical for the bourgeoisie, but his sacrifice deeply affected the people. His movement wasn't coincidental, it was a precursor of the revolutionary storm which was coming.

The uneven battle of Fikioris awakened first of all the farmers of Moria. The problems of the farmers were no less than those in Thessaly. There weren't large landowners, apart from a few exceptions. But the life of the farmers wasn't less miserable and poverty stricken. In three regions, Achaia, Ilias and Corinthia the main product were vines. The farmers had many small vineyards and in order to cultivate them they needed loans from moneylenders who looted the sweat and toil from the farmers. The farmers owed the moneylenders more than the value of their plots of land and many of those were mortgaged. The new class of capitalist which demanded power had already enraged the poor of the Peloponnese.

In 1894 a crisis of overproduction had developed in vines which lasted two decades. The farmers were sunk much deeper into desperation. There was discussion about creating cooperatives but the traders refused to even countenance the idea. They suffered their own disaster when the export of their produce was taxed at 15%. With the income of this tax they would fund the creation of a Bank so as to specifically combat this crisis.

They paid local newspapers to cultivate public opinion, they helped ministers and members of Parliament and they finally achieved in passing a Bill in Parliament. With this manoeuvre the traders were able to enrich themselves whilst the poor starved.

But the farmers didn't remain with their hands crossed. In 1903 in Pirgos and Patras they rose up and demanded to create a monopoly of wheat by the state. In Parliament Gounaris who was a personality of the old guard, a clever rhetorician and demagogue, using his talents attempted to trick the farmers and aid the traders. But in Moria and in other villages the slogan: Down with the old guard and we want a monopoly was heard.

Day by day the wind of resistance increased and in May of the same year the farmers organised armed contingents, one after the other. The farmers were threatening and they organised themselves shouting revolutionary slogans: Death to the Traitors, Death to the Exploiters, Monopoly Now! The government sent an army against them and many shots were fired. But the farmers didn't give up. Trampled upon and downtrodden in shabby clothes, angry and fierce from the conflict they picked up whatever tools they had and they attacked all the telegraph stations and train stations occupying them and destroying whatever they could lay their hands on.

From the insurrection Theotokis was forced to resign. But his problems were not over. Morias was still boiling…
Whilst these developments occurred in the countryside, the atmosphere in the cities was just as electric. Workers in Piraues and Athens sent messages to the King complaining about their economic situation. The traders also marched in the thousands in front of the Palace complaining about the endless and unjust taxes and the corruption of the aristocracy.

Everything showed that a revolution was coming. But its leadership -not its decisive vanguard - was the middle class of the bourgeoisie the traders, the industrialists and the officers of the army. But they themselves had been frightened by the distant noises of the revolution. In 1871 in France, the workers of Paris had risen up and occupied for a short period of time, state power. Their act which has remained in the history books and the Paris Commune, convulsed the world. In 1905 a new revolution in Russia created the phenomenon of the Soviets, those organs of proletarian power. A new era has arisen, the era of socialism. The Greek bourgeoisie could understand it could feel a cold chill down its spine. It was frightened the masses who might overthrow the old classes, wouldn't just stop there. Thus when the 1909 revolution broke out, the bourgeoisie ran to control it and direct it. They didn't let it wipe out parasitism once and for all.

The Goudi Movement

In the whole of Greece a situation of tense agony prevailed. Everyone thought that something would occur. Karaiskakis and the students issued proclamations, the Turks threatened Crete, the northern borders and the islands. The King threatened that if pressure is continued against him he would get his family and leave. Rallis who was the Prime Minister ordered two officers to be imprisoned. But the Union of Officers immediately decided to release both officers organising an escape. The mission was handed over to Pangalos. He helped organise it and the government and the Palace were shown up.

Rallis was in secret talks with the Union of Officers but after this event cut them off, throwing out with punches a representation of officers who had gone to his house for a visit. When the delegation of officers returned to the offices of the Union meeting was called and it was decided to declare a revolution in the night 14-15th August.

With an order from Zorba the army was called in Goudi. The officers higher up didn't dare to act. They locked themselves in their houses. The old order didn't have trust in its regime. Only one officer the colonel of the horse regiment Metaxas went to his regiment which was in

Goudi alongside another five officers from the horse regiment. The soldiers present didn't know that he wasn't a member of the Union, but Demestiha's men knew and they started to attack him as they knew he was from the Palace. A group got him and attacked him locking him up.

The above event ended without one drop of blood being spilt. But the Goudi revolution - as it was called - couldn't destroy the rotten parts of society. It started off with half-measures and ended with half-measures. This is quite clear from the programme which was published in the newspapers on 15 August 1909. The Union only wanted the removal of the royalist officers from the army and measures to improve the general standing of the army, services and the state in general.

Rallis understanding that the revolutionaries were soft tried to bargain and convince them. He couldn't as the conservative leaders of the Union of Officers were looked upon with distrust by the simple soldiers and the petty officers. When he saw he was getting nowhere he asked the King George to deal directly with Zorba. But the King was totally frightened he didn't want to see Zorba as he believed he would be arrested with this family. Thus the Rallis government was obliged to resign.

During the confusion the monarchist Kiriakoulis Mavromihalis who was quite an idiot wanted to by Prime minster and he notified the Administrative Committee of the Union, that he is willing to accept the Primeministership. Mavromihalis had an adviser who had studied economics.

Zorba replies to Mavromihalis and this became quite important. The programme of the union of officers must be accepted and the Rallis government must not dissolve itself before it votes in the new laws. Amnesty should be declared for all those involved in the movement. Mavromihalis replied that he accepts all the conditions but Zorba replies that he wants it written down. This was quite ridiculous as the all-powerful Revolution demanded amnesty from a shady government. And whilst Zorba was talking to Mavromihalis an even happened which we must refer to amongst the lower classes of the army with the leadership of the revolution.

Colonel Christodoulos had orders from Zorba to come from Halkidiki to Athens but they tried to go through Tatoi where there was a royal regiment. But a representative from the Palace said they couldn't go through. But Christodoulos who was famous for being hard swore at him and said it loudly so the soldiers heard. Christodoulos then ordered his soldiers to continue the course and they marched through the royal land.

When they arrived in Athens Zorba gave a speech regarding the aims of the Revolution and tried to calm them down. But when he left, not happy with what he heard, Christodoulos regarding amnesty and discipline stated "We have another bunch of weaklings here".

The Balkan Wars

When Venizelos forms a government many issues start to cloud over especially those of World War I. On the one hand the forces of the Triple Entente (England, France, Russia) and on the other those of the 'Central Empires' Germany, Austria are preparing with a war to re-divide the markets.

In the Balkans we had endogenous contradictions as the current states had not been wholly formed. Turkey still occupied very large areas. The Serbs, the Rumanians, the Bulgarians, the Greeks all fought against Turkey and each other in order to secure each the most favourable borders. They even fought to swallow up smaller nationalities like those of the Macedonians.

These inter-Balkan contradictions, were also aided from the interventions of the big power camps, who also are trying to place under their influence the Balkans and to take away the land of the sultans in Turkey.

In Greece these antagonisms are manifested with conflicts amongst the Kings successor, Constantine and Venizelos. The Kings successor is with the Kaiser and Venizelos alongside the ruling class he represents is on the side of the English and Entente. Despite all this Venizelos is obliged from the situation he is in to be loyal to the Palace and he places all the old guard in leading positions in the army such as Davsmani and Metaxas. When the first Balkan war breaks out in 1912 the Army is controlled by them.

In the first phase of the Balkan wars, the Greeks, the Bulgarian and the Serbs are allied to achieve a victory and to remove Turkey from the Balkans. But if we excuse Thessalonica, where the Greek army was able to occupy it, Epirus, Macedonia and Thrace were occupied by the armies of all the allies. In the bargaining's which followed the allies couldn't agree on the division of the land thus a new Balkan war broke out.

Greece, Serbia and Rumania with the support of the Entente went against Bulgaria who still looked favourably towards Turkey and was supported by the Austro-Germans.

In the meantime the Anglophile King George is murdered in a conspiracy organised by Austrian agents and we have on the throne the German supporter King Constantine.

From the Balkan wars which ended with the Treaty of Lausanne in Bucharest on 28th July 1913, the land mass of Greece increases from 64,000 square kilometres to 120,000 and its population from 1.8 million becomes 5 million. Another 500 kilometres of railways and 2,000 new roads. The state budget increased from 100 million gold drachmas and another 1228 new landholdings were added from Epirus and Macedonia.

The great achievements of the Greek army increased immensely the influence of Venizelos. Athens prepared to receive him after he returned from Bucharest. But he arrived secretly in the capital so as to prepare the arrival of the Chief of Staff King Constantine.

Venizelos hid from the people the stupid military mistakes of the royal general staff, which almost brought the Greek army to its knees. It's survival was only due to the diplomatic manoeuvres of Venizelos who from then was recognised internationally as a diplomatic personality.

When the 1st World War broke out, Venizelos wanted Greece to enter on the side of the Entente. But the English who themselves had as an aim to grab European Turkey and the Dardanelles, when Venizelos asked them for an alliance, replied to him that Greece would become acceptable only when the Anglo-French were attacked by the Turks.

In the meantime the correlation of forces in the Balkans changed. Rumania refused to carry out its military obligations and thus only Serbia remained alone against Bulgaria and Turkey.

The Anglo-French were in danger of seeing the Austro-Hungarians entering the Mediterranean. Thus they were obliged to ask for an alliance of Greece. But after the events surrounding Rumania started to hesitate. The Anglo-French promised him economic aid and armaments and they even said they would bring an Army to take over the Dardanelles. They sang in his ear the Great Greek song about occupying Constantinople and they asked him to enter the campaign with a force.

When Venizelos was finally convinced he had to confront the opposition of King Constantine and the generals he had placed in leading positions. King Constantine would have preferred the exit of Greece from the war on the side of the Central Empires and because this was impossible for him to achieve it, he limited himself to a policy of neutrality. He wasn't a peacemaker but he appeared as such, increasing his influence a little in opposition to Venizelos, who started to lose out due to his Entente friendly position and war mongering policy.

On September 11th the German Ambassador Mirbach visited King Constantine and he informed him as he had done previously with the Bulgarian government. "In the afternoon, Venizelos will bring me the declaration of war and general mobilisation, I will not sign it."

It is true when Venizelos visited him in Tatoi he let him develop his Entente friendly views and he finally replied to him in a sharp manner: "If the situation has changed, Bulgaria will fight with the Central Empire as an ally.

Germany will win and I don't want to be beaten by the Germans".

Venizelos was forced to impose his resignation. But Constantine was forced to offer his resignation. But Constantine didn't accept it. His throne was still in danger from this Cretan who still had an influence in the masses. He never forgot that his father George who hesitated in entering the first Balkan war, Venizelos said to him: "Your majesty, the war or your crown"!
He therefore signed the declaration. But it was this declaration which would bring about a collapse of Venizelos' influence. Immediately after its publication English forces arrived in Macedonia. In a short period of time French ones arrived as well and all the forces were under the joint command of the French officer General Sarai.

On the 21st September Venizelos spoke in Parliament about his war plans. The bourgeoisie who dreamed about Constantinople, power and wealth were enthusiastic. But the popular masses who were waiting for tragedies remained sceptical.

Constantine believed the time was now right to take revenge. He called Venizelos to the Palace and he declared with pride that he doesn't support his friendly to the war views. On 23rd September Venizelos submits his resignation and from now on the struggle amongst the ruling class and the oligarchy would gain large and bloody dimensions. The period of national division had firmly opened.

PART B
World War One and Greece

The 1821 Revolution against the Ottoman Empire laid the basis of the emergence of the Greek nation state, and hence bourgeois development. Greece's geographical position meant that it participated in the trade relations between Europe and the East. Without any levels of industrialisation "we can say that the role of Greek capitalism, was that of the middle man, a parasitic role, inside the overall functioning of international capitalism" (1)

From the middle of the 19th century onwards some heavy industry was built in Greece, but the country remained predominantly agricultural. The relations of Greek capitalism with foreign capital were such that Britain and

France dominated, but Russia and Germany were also involved in trade.

By 1909 with a peasant insurrection at Goudi there emerged the first steps towards bourgeois transformation of Greek society as the realms of the government were taken directly by an emerging Greek bourgeoisie. The period that was to follow was characterised by a development in industry, railroads, banking, insurance etc., as well as an extension of Greece's state borders during the 1912-13 Balkan wars.

The outbreak of world war one found Greece divided into two antagonistic camps, King Constantine I's monarchic government on the one hand and Venizelos (bourgeois liberal opposition) on the other. (2) Venizelos party was the main party of Greek capitalism and it organised disturbances in Thessalonica (1916) so as to forcefully make Greece participate in the war on the side of the Entente, despite King Constantine's neutralist stance.

By 1917-18 a relative development of Greek capitalism occurred due to the war (demand for war products as well as an increase in domestic production due to the Anglo-French embargo of 1915-16) as well as the extension of Greece's borders with the absorption of Macedonia, Thrace, Crete and the Aegean islands. By 1917 there were 110,000 employed workers who by 1920 had become 155,000. By 1917 52,000 were organised in trade-unions, by 1918 79,000 and by 1919 99,000. The population of Greece was around 7 million at the time.

But Greece remained predominantly an agricultural country as the peasants constituted 75% of the population. Large landholders still maintained control of one third of all the land and by 1917-18 in areas like Thessaly a peasant movement developed demanding redistribution of land. (3)

With the ousting of King Constantine I in 1917, Greece entered world war one on behalf of the Entente and so became a satellite to the great powers (Britain, France, Russia). The task confronting socialists was to oppose the war and call for the fraternisation of soldiers at the fronts. Instead of this the socialist parties adhering to the 2nd International sided with their respective governments, voted for war credits and thus betrayed proletarian internationalism. British, French and Russian socialists came into conflict with workers of the opposing battlefield under the slogans of a struggle for 'democracy', 'against Prussian militarism', 'against the Kaiser' etc.

Only the Bolsheviks in Russia, the Sparta cists in Germany and small internationalist groups in most countries maintained a Marxist attitude to imperialist war, which was further elaborated at Zimmer Wald and Kienthal.

Before world war one Greece had no socialist party or one unified trade-union movement. Various workers centres existed in Volos, Thessaloniki, Piraeus and socialist ideas were being propagated by localised socialist groups, but their influence was minute, if not insignificant. The outbreak of world war one changed all of this, although not immediately as most of the Greek socialists were largely inactive. As in other European countries the socialists became divided.

Various tendencies emerged:

a. Dracoulis's "Sosialistiko Kentro" (Socialist Centre) proclaimed it was a frie3nd of the Entente.

b. Giannos's "Socialistiko Kentro" (Socialist Centre) sided with Venizelos who campaigned for Greece's entrance on the side of the Entente.

c. Dimitratos's "Socialistiki Enosi" (Socialist Unity) did not take any clear anti-war stance.

d. Thessaloniki's "Federation" sided with King Constantine who was anti-Entente.

e. Ligdopoulos-Tzoulati "Socialistiki Neolaia tis Athinas" (Socialist Youth of Athens" founded in 1916 as a student group took a clear Marxist position against the war.

The paradox with other socialist parties in Europe was that the socialist movement was not united before the war or during it, but once it had ended.

At the 1st Pan-Hellenic Congress of Socialists (April 1915) no anti-war declaration was made. Nor did 'Socialist Unity' or the 'Federation' openly declare an opposition to the war. Their main priority were the 1915 elections and who to support, the King or Venizelos. Large demonstrations occurred during these elections with placards demanding 'Down with the War' and the 'Federation' took what it called a 'neutral' stance and ended up siding with the King. Dimitratos, Sideris and

Kouriel finally entered the coalition of the monarchic Gounaris in the same year.

An important Congress occurred in Budapest which established the Balkan Socialist Federation with socialist parties throughout the Balkans being called to make their positions clear in respect to the war. At this Congress (also in 1915) representatives from Rumania (Rakovsky), Serbia (Gerea, Dobrutsano), Bulgaria (Blagoev, Dimitrov, Kolarov) and Greece (Sideris) took part. Whilst the Congress took a clear internationalist stance against both imperialist blocks, being in the spirit of Zimmerwald. This was only as a result of a political struggle which occurred among the 'narrow' and 'broad' factions of the Bulgarian party, in which the latter was defeated and isolated for its social patriotic views on the war. Sideris, strangely enough was welcomed despite the fact that he had betrayed the workers by entering into Gounaris monarchic government whilst a member of the 'Federation'.

The Greek ruling class was divided in its response to the war, whilst the population seemed overall anti-war as a result of the tremendous casualties of the Balkan Wars of 1912-13. When Venizelos created a government in Thessaloniki, King Constantine retained his grip on Athens and as a result Britain and France who had used Greek soil to attack the Germans in Macedonia declared an economic embargo of Greece. Lenin characteristically noted:
"For which self-determination or 'independence' can one talk about - look - what they have done with 'independent' Greece...

Greece has been strangled by the Entente... taking by force part of Greek soil... Pressure by hunger has been imposed. Greece has been isolated by the warships of the Anglo-French and Russian imperialists Greece has been left without 'bread'.(4)

World war one provoked serious disturbances in a whole series of countries, where the working class agitated for an end to the war. In Greece the first signs of serious class struggle occurred in August 1916 when steelworkers in seriphos went on strike and were confronted by a lock-out and troops sent from Athens. Strikes also occurred by railroad workers in Larissa, sailors and shoemakers in Thessaloniki, Sira and Patras. Most importantly a general strike broke out in Volos which lasted for two months and was eventually crushed, whilst its repercussions were felt throughout the whole of Greece.

More importantly the impact of the February Revolution in Russia resulted in a shift by all Greek socialists towards the left and for unification. Two clear divisions started to emerge in the Greek socialist movement:

a) In most braches of the 'Socialist Party' social-patriotic positions were taken in support of the Entente. Its theses stated the following:

"After the fall of tsarism and the democratisation of Russia, the reactionary, semi-feudal and absolutist Hohenzollern monarchies of Germany, Austria and the Sultans remain the main enemies of the rights of nationalities and the freedom of the people in Europe. That the defeat of the Entente would mean an overthrow of the February Revolution and a possibility of a return of the Tsar and king Constantine with Prussian swords". (5)

At the 2nd Pan-Hellenic Congress of Socialists (July 1918) a decision was taken by all socialist groups to unify despite previous differences. Parallel with this development the labour movement was unified in November 1918 creating 'GSEE' (Greek Trade-Union Federation). Around 200 labour unions, from 20 cities representing 48 different occupations took part in the Socialist Congress, in all representing 60,000 workers from the 75,000 that were organised in unions.(6)

The Formation of the First Labour Party – SEKE

The Founding of the SEKE

The formation of Greece's first mass working class party with direct relations with the trade-union movement was an important step forward. At the founding congress 34 militants took part representing over 1,000 socialists. A few of the socialist groups are the following with their representatives:

'Federation' was represented by Benarogias, Antoniou, Arditis, Benroumbis.
'Sociaistiki Organosis'(Socialist Organisation) was represented by Komiotis, Petriskas, Danigos.
'Socialistiki Neolaia' by Ikonomou, Holmes.

'Ergatikos Agonas' (Workers Struggle) by Ligdopoulos.

Angel was elected President and he also became the official representative of the 2nd International. As is pointed out by Kousoulas, "The resolutions and the platform of the 1st Congress as well as the Charter of the Seke, showed no trace of Leninist influence; the Charter in particular, could have been that of any democratic party. The founders of the SEKE were well-intentioned idealists with commendable, albeit unrealistic, aspirations to rid the country of all social ills. In the following years the party they founded became, step by step, through crises, purges and intrigue, the present day Greek Communist Party, KKE". (7)

The founding documents expressed a social-democratic majority but three tendencies could be discerned:

a. The communist left led by Ligdopoulos, Tzoulatis, Komiotis.
b. The 2nd International centre led by Benarogias.
c. The right-wing led by Sideris, Giannos, Dimitratos.

The communist left voted against the idea at the Congress that the League of Nations was basically progressive wanting a real disarmament of nations. They also voted against the political programme of the new party which called for a Popular Democracy, and not a class based Soviet Democracy. Whilst being in a minority the communist left were able to pass a resolution in favour of the Russian Revolution. The Congress decided to join the 2nd International, but events worked against the decision with the founding of the 3rd International. 'Ergatikos

Agonas' (Workers Struggle was a socialist daily in Thessaloniki) became the official paper of the SEKE and Ligdopoulos it's editor.

The reasons behind the temporary gains of the communist left in achieving leading positions disproportionate to their size in the party can be explained by the fact that the right wing leaders wanted to use them for their own purposes. The pressure from the ruling class to subordinate militants and the leadership of the SEKE was great, but the pressure of the masses especially the youth towards the 3rd International was even greater, especially during an upturn in the movement. That is why the Congress decided not to be represented at the Stockholm Congress of the 2nd International.

After the Congress a struggle among the factions occurred. The communist left were called to implement the social democratic policies of the Congress and to publish its programme. Out of principle they refused to do this. In parallel behind the backs of the party Sideris, Kouriel and Dimitratos took part in the Socialist Congress of London and a scandal erupted revealing a block of the 'Federation' and Venizelos's government. They were then expelled from the party

In the meantime Venizelos's government arrested five members of the ruling council of GSEE who had sided with the SEKE, in order to frighten the strike wave which had erupted. But the strikes continued raising the demand for the release of the trade-union leaders. The SEKE intervened quite energetically in the strike wave and the government eventually gave in. just before the founding

Congress of the 3rd International the communist left decided to break from the SEKE and they sent Ligdopoulos as a delegate to the Balkan Federation in Sofia, which was later represented at the 3rd International. The right-wing leaders of the SEKE did not react immediately, sensing that nothing could stop the grassroots turn (i.e. the youth) in the party towards the Comintern. "Rizospastis" (Radical was an independent socialist daily in Athens which later became the official paper of the KKE) declared:

"The SEKE taking into account that the parties and organisations which comprise the 2nd International betrayed socialist ideology allying themselves with bourgeois government during war and in collaborating with them they have abandoned the class struggle, supported the imperialist war, gone against the fraternisation of peoples and the re-founding of a socialist international. We take note that the 2nd International which met in Verne and Amsterdam did nothing about the parties which betrayed the struggle and it is unable an impossible to overcome these policies with any necessary about turn.

The SEKE decides,

1. To leave the 2nd International and condemn its opportunist tactics.
2. Orders the Central Committee to prepare the groundwork for joining the Comintern and not to break off any relations with any parties of the 2nd International which have remained true to socialist principles".(8)

The right wing leadership did not accept the decision by the communist left to adhere to the 3rd International. Sideris, Kouriel and Dimitratos who had been expelled are reinstated. The communist left resigned in protest and their positions were taken by right wingers, who now decided not to adhere to any International.

The 2nd Congress of the SEKE in April 1920 overturned this decision and decided once more to adhere to the Comintern. The name of the SEKE was changed and the word communist was included in its brackets and this changed showed its contradictory nature. But the influence of social democracy ran very deep especially among its parliamentary deputies like Sideris and Kouriel who did not criticise the expansionist policies of Greek capitalism. The big political issues at the time was propaganda in defence of the Bolsheviks coupled with Greece's role in Asia-Minor and a turn towards the Comintern would have entailed a far greater level of anti-war propaganda and agitation which the right wing leaders of the SEKE would not have wanted. But overtures were made to Ligdopoulos and Tzoulatis who were then editing a journal called 'Kommunismos' (Communism) to rejoin the party. This group alone in Greece published at the time Lenin's 21 conditions of entrance into the Comintern, as well as the resolutions of its 1st and 2nd Congress, Marx's Capital, Lenin on Ultraletism, Kollontai on Family and Communism and a whole host of educational articles concerning Marxist economics and history. The police persecuted this group severely, smashing its headquarters and persecuting its members. Ligdopoulos and his comrades re-join the SEKE and he was sent to represent the party at the 2nd Congress of the Communist

International. But on his return he was murdered alongside the Russian Oikin (who was sent by the Bolsheviks) and any decisions taken in Moscow concerning the right wing leaders of the SEKE remain lost forever.

Asia-Minor Campaign

Venizelos sent troops which marched into northern Turkey in order to deal a blow to the nationalist movement of Kemal Ataturk and strengthen the strategic positions of British and French imperialism against Soviet Russia. The anti-Venizelos coalition of King Constantine stood in November 1920 elections on a programme of an end to the war, demagogically exploiting the desire of the population for peace. The SEKE also participated on an anti-war programme, but was unable to elect any MP's despite gaining 42,000 votes. This was mostly due to the unfavourable electoral system. When in power King Constantine continued the war seeking to occupy Ankara. By 1921 Greece's military adventures were failing its 'big power' allies sought a compromise with Kemal. Strikes broke out once more due to the economic effects of war (e.g. Tobacco workers, sailors, railroads etc.) and the SEKE(K) was faced with ever increasing state terrorism (smashing of its offices) due to its anti-war propaganda and its agitation for higher wages. Many militants as well as strikers were imprisoned or sent to the front and certain layers under pressure in the SEKE(K) leadership proposed a change in its political orientation.

The First Congress of the SEKE(K) which became known as the February Thesis (1922) signified an opportunist turn for the party. The "necessity for a long period of legality" was called by Georgiades and under conditions of harsh repression, this was a clear capitulation of Marxist principles. Georgiades speech was accepted by the Congress which elected Kordatos as secretary. His thesis was basically that capitalism had surpassed its post-war crisis and entered a period of stabilisation. On his return from the 3rd Congress of the C.I., Georgiades adopted the totally anti-marxist position of a "long period of legal activity, propaganda" (9) The C.I. under Lenin's and Trotsky's leadership had only affirmed signs of a relative improvements in the crisis.

By the summer of 1922 the crisis as a result of the continuing war led Gounaris' government to imprison all the members of the SEKE(K), the editor of 'Rizospastis' (which by now had become the official paper of the party) and the leaders of GSEE. Many Greek soldiers had been influenced by its anti-war propaganda and this led to a proposition being made to Kordatos for the SEKE(K) to enter the government and stop its anti-war propaganda. In replying to this proposal Kordatos wrote,
"General (referring to Metaxas) I thank you for the honour you have made. I recognise that the times through which the country is passing are critical. But as a member and secretary of the SEKE(K) I believe our role is not to save the throne or the bourgeois regime. We cannot take part in your government as our principles do not allow it". (10)
The eventual collapse of the Asia-Minor expedition led to many minor insurgencies, but not to revolution. Various committees were formed calling themselves soviets, but

they lacked any spontaneity or popular support, being mostly organised from above by militants. (11)

An Extraordinary Congress was convened in October 1922 and Sargologos was elected secretary till the summer of 1923. It later became known he was an agent provocateur. During his reign most of the decisions of the February Thesis were overturned and Georgiades alongside Benariogas were expelled. Kordatos remained in the leadership and the new orientation of the party was summed up as being: elections based on proportional representation, repeal of martial law, occupation of large landholdings without compensation, trade-union unity, united front against the lowering of wages, peace, self-determination for the minorities, for factory committees and a Workers and Peasants Government. In other words the SEKE(K) was politically orientated towards the decisions of the 4th Congress of CI. But the party, in the crucial years of 1923-24, like elsewhere in Europe, failed in practically implementing these policies.

When Gonatas government in August 1923 decreased all wages by 20%, the entire labour force of 150,000 went on strike. General Plastiras unleashed a violent anti-working class backlash using the army and declaring martial law. The SEKE(K) took an energetic part in the strike with less than 1,000 militants was instrumental in making the general strike possible, through Maximos (a CC member) who was the main strike coordinator.

But the strike did not lead as expected to a change in the balance of class forces favourable to the workers. No workers defence squads were created, no sections of the army were won over, in practice the masses did not prepare for an immediate seizure of power.

The general strike was violently crushed by Plastiras, with numerous deaths. The basic causes of its defeat were analysed by the SEKE(K) new secretary Apostolides in "Rizospastis" (26 August 1923) as being the result of divisions which emerged in labour in the labour movement when the rail workers and postal workers unions decided to end their strike. But the party did not as one would have expected criticise its own responsibilities in:

a. Calling for a mass demonstration in Piraeus where no government offices existed
b. Underrating the significance of the movement and its pre-revolutionary character.
c. Not agitating for workers defence guards.
d. Not condemning the separate negotiations of the rail workers and postalwokers unions to end the strike.

Two months after the outbreak of the strike general Metaxas organised a coup on 21st September 1923. The SEKE(K) leadership now called on the masses to support Plastiras as opposed to the monarchist Metaxas. The argument behind such a mistaken policy was that Metaxas was Kornilov whilst Plastiras was Kerensky. The reality was totally different, as Plastiras was a military general, not a bourgeois liberal democrat like Kerensky. In the meantime Metaxas coup disintegrated, Plastiras called for new elections. The SEKE(K) despite the fact that it stood more candidates, received only 20,000 votes out of an electorate of 800,000. An explanation for this dramatic fall of over half its previous total is due to the election rigging of Plastiras and the incoherent policies of the SEKE(K), which during this period defended bourgeois instead of socialist democracy. For instance,

"We are followers of social democracy. But now we will underrate the importance of social democracy and will struggle to impose, with the majority of the people always, a west-european type of democracy, without a monarchy". (12)

At the end of 1923, Pouliopoulos as leader of the "Enosis Paleonpolemioston" (War Veteran's Union) travelled to Moscow. Parallely a whole series of militants arrived on board the vessel Chicherin, like Sklavos, Zachariades, Skitalis, Arvanitakis, Nikolaides, Sakarelos etc., who were all graduates of the Communist University of Eastern Peoples (KUTV). There were taught Russian as well as Marxism, history, economics etc. They all essentially formed the basic nucleus of Stalinism in Greece. As noted by Kousoulas the,

"Kutvies' were trained Russian speaking Communists whose loyalty to Stalin was to play an important role in the following years… their intimate contracts with the Soviet Embassy in Athens, implying that they were trusted more than the regular party leaders, were a constant source of irritation…" (13)

The divisions among Stalin's and Trotsky's factions emerged at the start of 1924 in "Rizospastis" which published a series of articles by Karageorgis attacking the Left Opposition.

On the 3rd February 1924 the SEKE(K) convened its National Congress to analyse the downturn in the movement. The situation which it found itself in was contradictory as:

a. Pouliopoulos tendency started to emerge,
b. The party underwent a crisis which was related with the impact of the Thermidor in the USSR and a Greek troika emerged.

In order to solve the crisis an anti-democratic resolution was voted by all the factions, which stated:
"1) It is impossible for the party to develop as a political organism of the working class if the crisis is not resolved.

1. The great enemy of the party… are the internal opportunist elements anarchic in thought, anti-communist in essence… and those chiefly responsible are the reformers.

So as to confront decisively the two enemies it is necessary for there to exist in the leadership of the party a small directorate which having the necessary minimum of homogeneity and having absolute power when necessity arises to override the constitution"(14)

The Greek troika was centred around Apostolides, Maximos, Kordatos and after this resolution was taken, expelled the whole of the branch of Piraeus. (15) Many militants associated with the journal 'Archives of Marxism' were also expelled, as was its main leader Tzoulatis, despite the fact of being in the national council of the SEKE(K). See Chapter on the Archeiomarxist movement.

The Congress did not refer to the interjections of the Comintern's representative A.Petrovsky due to reasons of security. But the expulsions did show that the triumvirate in Moscow, Zinoviev, Kamenev and Stalin sought to have their influence imposed on the leadership of the SEKE(K). This they achieved.

When a plebiscite was called by Papanastasiou for April 1924, for democracy or a monarchy, the SEKE(K) took part voting yes to 'democracy'. A letter was sent to the Prime Minster,
"emphasising that our participation in the plebiscite seeks to conclusively bury monarchism and a general explanation to the workers and peasant masses will occur explaining what bourgeois democracy is". (16)

Democracy finally won in the plebiscite, but that did not stop Papanastasiou enforcing anti-working class measures like his predecessors.

When the GSEE called a Mayday demonstration in 1924, the army was called to disperse the workers. Slogans such as 'Long Live Red Mayday', 'Long Live the Russian Revolution, the Dictatorship of the Proletariat' dominated, while the Internationale was also sang. But when too many workers refused to disperse, the 'democratic' forces intervened killing one and injuring many.

Not long after a new strike wave erupted, despite the defeat of 1923. Dockers were the first to go on strike followed by tobacco workers, railroads, electricians, seafarers, workers in the port of Elefsina etc. Despite an international upturn in the economy, Greece's economic crisis deepened, mostly due to the influx of refugees from the ending of the Asia-Minor expedition and an agricultural crisis (due to the lack of any new machinery, high taxes etc.) The expelled branch of Piraeus (Papanastasiou, Arvanitakis) led the strikes there calling for an occupation of the ships. The official party considered this call 'extremist'. The SEKE(K) failed to build from this new strike wave. The masses were undoubtedly ahead of the party. The union of Piraeus gave fierce battles but left on their own they eventually lost. The SEKE(K) had been crippled by expulsions, its militants were in disarray and it proved itself incapable of meeting the demands of the labour movement. Eventually the strike wave of 1924 was beaten. Strikers were court martialled all over Greece, in Drama, Kavalas, Thessaloniki, Athens and it ended in June 1924.

The Founding of the KKE (Greek Communist Party)

The 5th congress of CI was held in Moscow in July 1924 and it centred on the German issue. Zinoviev, now its main leader, totally misjudged the German situation, seeing revolution just round the corner. Dimitrovs CP in Bulgaria also proved unable to counter the backlash against his party and the insurrection it attempted in Neva Zagora was mercilessly crushed. Kolarov, the new secretary of CI submitted a resolution on the Balkans whereby the nascent CP's had to orientated themselves towards autonomists nationalists and peasant leaders. Trotsky quite correctly wrote about this turn stating,
"The Stalinists started to seek freshly made forces outside the proletariat idealizing the pseudo-peasant parties, flirting with Randitz and Lafollette the international

overestimates the peasants instead of the red unions, having faith in the leadership of the unions, the friendship with Chiang KAI-SHEK the Kuomintang is above classes etc."

The alliance of Bulgaria's CP with the autonomists Alexandrov and Panitsa and the adoption of the slogan for a" United and independent Macedonia and Thrace led to serious problems for the KKE. Kolarov, Manuilinsky and Zinoviev demanded that the Greek delegates adopt this slogan. Macedonians became a geographical area without taking into account the concrete composition of the nationalities that lived there, especially after the influx of the 700.000 Greeks as a result of the Treaty of Lausanne. A Thracian nationality was arterially created. In Greece national problems existed for the slavomacedonians, the ottomans of Western Thrace , The pomaks. One could not be termed a communist if they did not fight the depression of their " own country" against the various national minorities. But these nationalities were on the whole ignored.

The situation in the Balkan CP's became the following: The Yugoslavian CP refused to accept the Kosovo province was Albanian and ignored the self-determination of the Croats, Slovaks, Slavomacedonians. The Rumanian CP said nothing granting Dobroutsas to Bulgaria and the Hungarian minority in Transylvania. The Albanian socialists said nothing about the Greek minority in southern Albania. The Greek CP had no concrete slogans for the national minorities oppressed by the Greek state.

The Bulgarian CP had no time for the Slavomacedonians.
Not without reason, Lenin once asserted that opportunism
on the national question was the worst of all.

Maximos as leader of the Greek delegation at the 5th
Congress of the CP criticised the positions of Kolarov and
Manuilinsky in the following manner :
"The Greek section has always supported the just demands
of the national minorities which live in Greece and their
self-determination. But the slogan for a ""United and
Independent Macedonia and Thrace" is unrealisable. As
inside this geographical no particularly united national
minority existed and because the composition of the
populations of Macedonia and Thrace after the influx of
refugees was totally Greek. The Greek element was more
than the Muslims of Eastern Thrace and the
Slavomacedonians of Western Macedonia. No particular
Thracian nationality existed" (18)

Maximos added that the slogan "United and Independent
Macedonia and Thrace" may aid the Bulgarian
Communists, but no the Greek ones. Manuilsky went to
the criticise the Greek delegation as right-wing
opportunists and the SEKE(K) as clear opportunists.

The 3rd Extraordinary Congress was held from Nov-Dec
1024 whereby the KKE was founded. The Kremlin its
most numerous delegation composed of 5 members , more
than was even sent to the large parties of Europe, all with
the right to vote (Manuilinsky from the CI, Smeral from
the Czechoslovakian CP and executive member of the CI,
delegates from the French and Italian CP's as well as the
Balkan Federation.) The Kremlin wanted to control the

KKE , it being the strongest party in the Balkan's after the defeat of the Bulgarian CP. As well as the fact that most of the KKE's leaders like Apostolidis, Kordatos, Petsopoulos, Stavridis, and Pouliopoulos had shown such opposition on the national question.

The congress criticised vehemently the Apostolidis, Maximos and Kordatos leadership, but did not dare criticise the CI or the BALKAN Federation. No analysis of the German or Bulgarian defeats were made or Maximos's leadership during the defeat of the Greek general strike of 1923 and the strike wave in 1924. But most importantly no discussion occurred concerning the developments in the USSR after Lenin's 'death, especially the conflict among the troika and Trotsky.

The congress also adopted a policy of 'bolshevisation' for the KKE which the 5th Congress of the CI had called : "The Congress adopts unanimously all the resolutions of the CI Congresses as well as those of the Balkan Federation, especially the decisions of the 2nd Congress of the CI and Lenin's 21 conditions for acceptance into the 3rd International. In accordance with these conditions the Congress agrees to change its name from SEKE to KKE (19).

Pouliopoulos due to this position as leader of the War Veterans Union and his Zinovievite leanings was elected secretary at the youthful age of 24. In practice the 'bolshevisation' of the KKE turned out to stalinisation just like the 'Lenin Levy' was in the USSR. The KKE attempted to replace the rotten liberalism of its social democratic past with leninist democratic centralism. As noted by Kousoulas,

"The cell composed of the 3 to 5 members, offered the organisational framework for the total utilisation of the members. In such small groups one could escape notice by losing himself in the crowd. The cells, integrated in a closely knit structure, permitted the close supervision of party members. Such cell were to be formed at the factories and the shops where people spent most of their working hours. In addition party members belonging to labour unions should form 'factions' 'in each union local'.'(20)

But Leninist democratic centralism was never introduced, instead a regime of bureaucratic centralism whereby every ideological struggle was stifled and trampled upon alongside basic members rights, such as the right to criticise, control, show initiative. A regime of monolithism slowly emerged whereby everyone voted "yes" to everything the leadership proposed.

The CI did not confront any ideological issues but simply sought to subdue and make the CP's dependent on it. It replaced leaders and expelled thousands in the struggle against trotskyism. The CP's were subdued- the Greek one was no exception- becoming obedient organs of Stalin. Under Pangalos's dictatorship war was declared on the workers and peasant and more than 1.000 members of the KKE were arrested, its leadership mostly in exile or in prison. The main accusation for this rabid anticommunism was the KKE's stance on the national question whereby it was asserted that it wanted to hand over Greek land to the Bulgarians.

But most importantly serious conflicts emerged between the workers and the state and especially serious was the tobacco workers strike and the peasants insurgency demands for the expropriation of large landowners were made. The KKE look an energetic part, especially its militants in The War Veterans Union in Supporting the peasants but certain political capitulations were made to peasant leaders in creating dangerous illusions about their revolutionary potential. But the biggest political mistake of all was when Pangalos coup occurred and the KKE considered him a " progressive officer". POULIOPOULOS WHO WAS IN EXILE AT THE TIUME, CRITICISED THIS OPPORTUNIST POLICY AND THE FIRST OF INTERNAL SPLIT INSIDE THE KKE STARTED TO EMERGE. But it was during this period that the Stalinists started to take control of the party leadership.

When Pangalos demanded the closure of "Rizospastis" and the KKE leaders faced the death penalty over their stance in Macedonia and Thrace , Pouliopoulos at the trial which was to make the KKE famous throughout the whole of Greece defended with vigour the CI line asserting.

"The KKE is for the self-determination of peoples . The principles is the only one which has inspired the KKE in its different activity. It is totally impossible and illogical to accept that it is possible for us to cooperate with the blood drenched regime of Tsangov, who has shot and murdered thousands of communists in Bulgaria". (21)

At the trial of Sargologos who was an ex-secretary of the party was a witness for the prosecution. The trial was finally adjourned indefinitely as public opinion was too strong to close down "Rizospastis" and sentence to death the leaders of the KKE, who were sent to internal exile.

When Pangalos' dictatorship was overthrown by a new military coup led by the Venizelist officer Kondilis , The KKE made another turn in support and the KKE leaders faced the death penalty over their stance in Macedonia and Thrace , Pouliopoulos at the trial which was to make the KKE famous throughout the whole of Greece defended with vigour the CI line asserting.

"The KKE is for the self-determination of peoples . The principles is the only one which has inspired the KKE in its different activity. It is totally impossible and illogical to accept that it is possible for us to cooperate with the blood drenched regime of Tsangov, who has shot and murdered thousands of communists in Bulgaria". (21)

At the trial of Sargologos who was an ex-secretary of the party was a witness for the prosecution. The trial was finally adjourned indefinitely as public opinion was too strong to close down "Rizospastis" and sentence to death the leaders of the KKE, who were sent to internal exile.

When Pangalos' dictatorship was overthrown by a new military coup led by the Venizelist officer Kondilis , The KKE made another turn in support of him when a general amnesty of all political prisoners was declared. Kondilis was now considered a " progressive officer" and this was justified at the time as an article argued many years later, "the mystery of Kondilis democratisation must be sought in his place of exile, in Folegandros and Santorini where he had been sent by Pangalos's dictatorship. There influenced by exiled communists he changed his fascist views". (22)

A political struggle against such totally absurd views which were put forward by the emerging stalinist faction of Haitas, Zachariadis , Eftihiadis and Stavridis was initiated by Pouliopoulos and Maximos.

When certain "monarchist officers" led by Zervas and Derdilis sided against Kondilidis, the KKE lent practical support to Kondilis, instead of siding against all the bourgeois militarists. The KKE became a participant in the ensuing feud between the monarchic and "democratic" faction of the ruling class-siding with the "democrats". It thus left no room for independent class politics arguing incorrectly against a strategy which could have led them to power,
"if monarchism did not achieve its plan in taking power in yesterday's crucial battles that is due to the real forces in the country of workers, peasants and the politics of our party. We have never hidden the fact that as a revolutionary party our strategic aim is the conquest of power. That is our tactics based on today's reality excludes an immediate struggle for power, not even talk about it.(23)

When elections were held in November 1926 the KKE stood alongside peasant and refugee candidates gaining 11 MP's (42.000 votes) while Venizelos Liberals gained 143 MP's and Monarchist Republicans 127 MP's. Divisions erupted in the KKE's parliamentary faction over the Macedonian issue, as the majority of its MP's (8 out to 11) supported by Pouliopoulos faction. Venizelos's Liberals tried to utilise these divisions for their own anti-communist purposes by rescinding parliamentary immunity of the KKE's MP's, but the oppositionist MP's correctly concealed these divisions for their class enemy. In the meantime Pouliopoulos has resigned as general secretary and a deep internal crisis broke out in the KKE : See Appendix B

A new leadership was 'elected' without the participation of hundreds of members of the KKE around Haitas Eftihiades Sklavou and Tsatsakou, with Giatsopoulos as secretary (who soon sided with the opposition). They organised a 'pre-discussion' period for the KKE's 3rd Congress. At this Congress, the CI representative characterised the "policies of the KKE as right-wing".(24)

Especially harsh were the characterisations against Pouliopoulos tendency who were viewed as "capitulators". Maximos was elected secretary (he soon joined the opposition) and Pouliopoulos as well as Giatsopoulos were expelled for publishing the document " Neo Xekinima" and more than 500 members were soon expelled.

During 1927 a serious tobacco workers strike occurred by 40,000 who were locked out by the government. Street battles occurred in Xanthi, Thessaloniki, Kavala and elsewhere. The strike was finally betrayed when GSEE agreed to dissolve all unions which belonged to the KKE, making an agreement with the minister Tsaladaris that all arrested strikers will be set free allowed to work again. The KKE stance during the strike which was not revolutionary, it's aptly described by Stinas a leading functionary of the party in the 1920's.

"Two, three days after the strike breaks out, Maximos come to Kavalas. He calls the party branch which led the union and announced the decision of the Politburo. The strike must assume the character of simply not going to work...' In a few days Theo in Kavala announcing the new decision of the Politburo.

'The strike must become militant.' A demonstration of the strikers is called (more than 12.000) in an atmosphere of enthusiasm and the decision is taken for a militant way forward. Suddenly the next day Theos proposes to save the chief of Police. All the members are against this. We have nothing to do with him. The workers are preparing for the battles and leaflets which call for a demonstration the next day. Theos insists.

He asserts that he is responsible and he is the one who should finally decide. Before the bloody events erupt and under of the chief of police, with the special credentials of a man who has the final word, he orders that the leaflets should not be distributed and all demonstrations to be called off. This strike-breaking stance by Theos was never discussed or condemned. All the times that comrades insisted on a discussion the reply was that a public discussion and condemnation would aid the 'capitulators'.(25)

Third-Period Stalinism.

The KKE's influence of GSEE was up until 1927 quite
strong, when GSEE decided to affiliate to the 2nd
International. The KKE then set up 'action committees' in
an attempt to break the workers from the GSEE. This
ultimatist approach led the KKE for which it was criticised
by Pouliopoulos, to creating a new separate union called
the EGSEE. They ended up calling demonstrations which
were poorly attended. Workers did not leave their unions
because the KKE's leaders throughout that the beast way
to combat reformism was to ignore it and set up parallel
unions , thus dividing the working class.

When the 6th Congress of the CI (Jul-Aug 1928) occurred
it adopted Stalin's basic ideas at the time: the theory of
socialism in one country, the theory of social fascism, the
theory of the third and last stage of capitalism etc. The 4th
Congress of the KKE which occurred in late 1928
unanimously adopted all these positions and attempted to
implement them in Greece.

At the Congress the United Opposition of Maximos,
Sklavos, Hainoglou etc., were expelled. The fall in the
electoral strength of the KKE when it stood in the elections
(August 1928) , gaining only 14.000 votes was not
analysed. Haitas was elected secretary, signifying the
official acceptance of stalinism in its ultra-left period.

During the period 1928-30 the methods of struggle among
the workers organisations reached a tremendously low
level;, damaging the movement itself, especially after
Venizelos's democratic government passed a law banning

communist agitation. The KKE due to the publicity it has archived was able quite easily to spread lies against its political opponents calling them "archeiofascists", "socialfascists", "counter-revolutionaries", "capitulators".

"Rizospastis" reported in a near enough daily basis on the "method" of the Archeio-marxists, that they used to hit workers, dissolve unions and meetings. But the reality was the opposite. "In the trade unions, factories , public meetings, wherever the stalinist KKE was in a majority, all oppositionists were denied the right of free speech. But the fact that oppositionists were not always that numerically weaker meant that members of the KKE were confronted on a physical level as well. Here are a few examples of the "Rizospastis" used to write:

"The social fascists and capitulators are common agents of the tobacco owners".(26)

"Archeio-marxists with clubs and knives were waiting on a street corner to murder workers. Because of the dark they attacked three of their own fascists."
This should read as an attack organised by the stalinists.(27)

"In Volos three workers revealed to management the archeiofascists Stamba who was working at Damianos factory and he soon fired."(28)

A common tactic at the time was to reveal to the boss of a factory who oppositionists were, calling them communists, anarchists, etc. so they could be fired.

"Armogenis, Kapetanakis, Barchambos, and Sideropoulos are leaders of the fascist organisation called Archeio in Agrinio and they attempted to take over the leadership of the local trade-unions".(29)

The methods of Stalinism, which reached the point of murder, flowed from the theory whereby social democracy was considered a worse enemy than fascism and that is how the Archeio-Marxists and the Spartakos opposition were seen. This 'strategy' eventually led in Germany in 1933 to Hitler's rise to power and in Greece to Metaxas dictatorship in 1936. The forces of the labour movement were divided and weakened in the struggle against fascism and on these divisions fascism gained the upper hand.

Stalin's methods against the Left Opposition would eventually lead to the infamous show trials of the 1930's whereby all Lenin's co-workers would be imprisoned or shot. The KKE, like every other CP in the world at the time, repeated Stalin's lies and supported him till his death uncritically and passionately.

By 1930 the KKE had entered an utterly degenerate phase which threatened it with dissolution. A major role in the process was the fact that the KKE decided to call for a "general political strike, of armed demonstrations of working masses, of the peasantry and mass action by the sailors"(30)

When the movement was extremely weak. The CI referred to this period in the following manner,

"The leadership of the party is extremely weak. It has made a whole series of opportunist mistakes. A whole series of strikes and mobilisations of the workers and peasants have occurred without any involvement of the party's leadership. The party has 1.500 members, its influence in the industries has fallen. The minimum of the readers of the party's press which in June of last year 3.000 has now fallen to 1,666. In Athens the Party has 170 members and in Piraeus 70. Passivity in the national questions. Until today the party has done no practical activity in the oppressed masses. It remains satisfied simply with the slogan "United and Independent Macedonia and Thrace". Inside the Politburo in which two months ago no disagreements exists, two groups have appeared which are struggling against each other. We are convinced that among them no such serious political differences justify inter-party struggle"(31)

Possibly the greatest single factor which maintained the KKE united was surely the grandeur of the 'socialist' motherland, the USSR. Both of the leading tendencies, named Haisa-Eftihiadis, were criticised as being "right wing" and Theos' , Siantos . Piliotis as being "left wing deviationists", being involved in a 'factional struggle without principles'. Stalin's politics concerning the theory of the third and last stage of capitalism, of social fascism, of the forcible expulsion of communists, in conclusion of dividing the working class, were <u>undoubtedly correct and were not criticised.</u>

The crisis in the KKE was not seen as a by-product of the whole previous political history of Stalin's CI, but essentially because of the strangle among two basically stalinist groupings. The end result was that by 1931 the CI used both tendencies as a scapegoat for its own mistaken policies and Zachariades was elected secretary of the KKE, a position he maintained for the next quarter of a century. Two major decisions he presided over were:

i. 6th Plenum of KKE (1934) – No longer was it necessary to have a socialist, only a bourgeois democratic revolution in Greece.

ii. Rise of the KKE due to the German occupation during WWII, led to historic betrayal at Varkiza(1945) where the KKE agreed to disarm its partisan guerrillas and was them embroiled in a civil war until 1949 which it lost.

Conclusion

Any historical analysis of the early years of Greek Communism cannot but take into account the relative backwardness of Greek society, economically, politically, and culturally. WWI provoked a serious crisis in the ruling class as well as in the proletarian and peasant movement. The Russian Revolution in turn led a radicalisation of the masses which resulted in:

a. the unification of the trade-unions
b. the formation of Greece's first mass working class party.

The fact that no historical tradition of social democracy existed, no classic works of marxism were published before 1917, led the emerging labour movement to join the 2nd International at a time of its severe crisis. The formation of the 3rd International had a deep impact among the young militants of the SEKE who were inspired by Lenin's anti-war policies. The war against the nationalist Kemal and the young Soviet republic by the Greek bourgeoisie monarchist and 'democratic' led the problems both at the front as well as at home. Young soldiers and workers were attracted to the SEKE's anti-war propaganda and activity. Attempts by the SEKE's left-wing to place it firmly in the camp of communism were continually undermined, but never totally reversed. The repressive nature of all Greek governments' in the 1920's in practice meant that only a party which was prepared to act under illegal conditions had a hope of gaining the allegiance of the workers. It was logical therefor that Greeks militants aspired to the traditions of bolshevism and no other.

But when in the space of a few years the ideals of the Russian Revolution degenerated alongside important defeats of the proletariat on an international scale these in turn had an impact on the combativity of the Greek proletariat. The failures of the general strikes in 1923-4 led to Pangalo's dictatorship, which near enough smashed the KKE. Its own political mistakes especially over the issue of Macedonia and Thrace, were made by inexperienced young cadres who followed loyally every twist and turn of the Comintern's policies. On the whole this was due to the prestige which the communists had gained during the revolution and civil war that followed. As correctly pointed out by Trotsky,
"If someone were to check the names of delegates at the first four Congresses, in other words those first friends of the October Revolution, the most committed, the founders of the Communist International, Lenin's direct co-workers

on an International level he will find with few exceptions that they all after Lenin's death , were not only removed from the leadership, but were also expelled from the Communist International. This is true not only for the Soviet Union but for France, Greece, Italy the Scandinavian countries, Czechoslovakia,- true not only for Europe- but also and for America".(32)

The history of the Communist movement in Greece proves no exception to this process.

The question which now has to be asked was whether the Greek working class was really capable of demanding state power, in an overwhelmingly peasant based economy. No simply yes or no answer can be given. But if the KKE's militants had not betrayed a whole series of strikes , if they had not made political capitulations to a whole host of dictators and finally if they had not divided the labour movement on the basis of 'social fascists' and anti-trotskyist propaganda the possibility did exist for the KKE to break out of its isolation. Even more so if it had united with the militants of Archeio-Marxists who had made significant inroads into proletarian centres, like Piraeus. The KKE could have then reversed the persecutions against the Left in general and under conditions more favourable fought to take power. But like everywhere else in Europe at the time, Stalin made sure that was not to be.

VN Gelis
July 1999

Part C
The Macedonian Question: Balkan Stalinism and the National Question

The struggle of Galvinov against the Federation and Benagoria for their opportunism against the national question was also a struggle against the leadership of the 2nd International and Rakovsky who had allied themselves with the view that the movement of the Neo-Turks (young Turks) was progressive at the time when the proletariat was entering the arena, but also that national self-determination was possible within the framework of the Ottoman Empire.

From their point of view the slavomacedonians of Bulgarian area of Pirin had made the Komitatsides Macedonians Alexandrov, Protogerov and Panitsa into national heroes having set up a mausoleum for them in Agios Oros (where there is a church recently opened by Mitsotakis in the interests of American friendship). There news reports referred to the fact that strange developments were occurring between monks and citizens with aims which are not particularly irrelevant with the explosive situation in the Balkans.

Comrade Pandelis Pouliopoulops ignored this given existence of the Slavomacedonian nationality and organization and organization and his report did not speak about a 'Macedonian Nationality' about the 'Macedonian people' and the right for their self-determination.
The slogan 'United and Independent Macedonia and Thrace' was the only one as if there weren't other

nationalities which have need for their national liberation inside the Balkans, or inside Greece, Cyprus.

'There are clear manifestations which show us the existence of a consciousness of the Macedonian people' Pouliopoulops declared. But which Macedonian peoples? "A section of the Macedonian people has been organized in EMEO and is demanding with a show of arms to return to their homes" he continued. We were dealing with a few thousand Bulgarian Macedonians of Pirin who had already been exchanged with Greeks in Bulgaria. The other occupants of Macedonian refugees and Greeks were characterized as being Macedonians!!!

Pouliopoulos was trapped by the Kremlin and adopted the slogan of the 'United and Independent Macedonia and Thrace' and defended it as if it wasn't part of the Komitatsides and of Bulgarian capitalism, a slogan. Later Pouliopoulos in the 'Neo Xekinima' characterized the slogan 'Foolish and opportunistic'.

This slogan was un-geographical as there was no particular Macedonian nationality. As there was no Thracian one either.

In Thrace there exists and still exists an issue of the Turkish-Muslim nationality, which as oppressed by Greek capitalism could have the democratic right of their liberation and Independence.

This slogan was a technical creation which based on geographical criteria- and not ethnological- which on their own do not make a nationality. But this slogan: 'United and Independent Macedonian and Thrace' was not only un-geographical. It was also opportunist.

"Marx-Lenin emphasized- does not on its own create such national movements. But when such movements are formed and lead the masses communists attempt to divert the influence of the bourgeois class and the petty bourgeois leadership and to turn them towards the workers socialist movement".

It was the Mensheviks who believed that the weight of the democratic demands as that of peasant reform, the self-determination and independence of the people from the great Russian generally presupposes the leadership of the coming revolution from the bourgeois class, a thing which transformed the Mensheviks into followers and servants of the bourgeois class.

Marx gave initial importance to the workers movement as the only movement able for the independence of the oppressed nations. Instead the followers of the slogan 'United and Independent Macedonia and Thrace' of the Committal of the troika was collaborating with the petty bourgeoisie and the bourgeoisie of EMEO, programmatised unity in one party with them.
'Marx did not transform the national movements into something which was absolute knowing full well that only the victory of the proletariat could free forever all the nationalities' (Lenin : The Utopian Marx and the Practical R. Luxembourg)

"Social democracy -wrote Trotsky- unites the solution of the current problems into realms of the creation and the formation of nation states, cannot move forward the principle of national self-determination which in the last analysis appears as the recognition of the right of every national group to decide about the fate of its state, consequently for the right of the peoples to leave a given state as is by plebiscite' (May 1917)

Only the plebiscite which constitutes a democratic right for the communists could show if a Macedonian nationality exists wanted they say to achieve its independence. But neither did the C.I. or the Balkan Federation consider it necessary to argue for a plebiscite regarding their directive on Macedonia!

Pouliopoulos knew all this but due to the opportunist decisions which were talked on the Macedonian question at the 5th Congress ignored the multinational conditions of the Macedonian area in which the most people were the Greeks and did not ask for a plebiscite to receive a true picture of the nationalities which occupied "Macedonia". The result of the report which Apostolides did for the Central Committee to ascertain there existed a Macedonian nationality was negative. It was a catapult against the loyal followers of the slogan for the ind3ependence of Macedonia and Thrace. Not one cell in Macedonia and Thrace accepted this slogan.

The slogan for the United and Independent Macedonia and Thrace was opportunist as they placed its solution within the framework of capitalism and they cut it off from the perspective of the socialist revolution.

Lenin did not disagree the independence of a nationality oppressed within the framework of capitalism. But emphasized that only within a regime of constant bourgeois democracy could that be resolved up until a certain point . In such a case direct subjugation would not become indirect.

In the period of imperialism the international labour movement writes on its flag the unresolved national problems as that of national self-determination and independence, and resolves them through the socialistic revolution and thus the bourgeois democratic revolution becomes socialist and thus it becomes permanent. Pouliopoulos differentiated himself with respect to this question from the representative of the Communist International, discreetly.

They allied the task of national liberation with that of social liberation and alongside that of the Balkan Socialist Federation.

But in the end they voted for the slogan which signed with the Komitatsides, Kolarov, Manuilinsky and the Kremlin of the Troika. That was the era when everyone voted exactly whatever Moscow said or did. Pouliopoulos in order to support the un-geographical slogan of the independence of Macedonia used an unacceptable argument.

The threat of a new war he said, is immediate, Macedonia is threatened by Bulgaria (exit to the Aegean) and from Serbia (views on Thessaloniki) Behind these states are hidden the imperialists of France, Italy.

'We will therefore provide the only solution against the war.'

What would this solution be about the stopping of the war, the independence of Macedonia and Thrace. It would provoke the intervention of Bulgaria and Serbia to add them.
Is it not capitalism which gives birth to war? What happened with the principle that only the socialist revolution constitutes an exit to the war. Marxism distinguish the position of the proletariat from the position of the bourgeois class and the parties above the national question. Not only in the country which oppresses another nationality but also the country which is being oppressed. But all the defenders of the 'Macedonian' did not stop in accepting the cooperation with the bourgeois leaders of EMO, with those who allied themselves with the murderer of the masses Tsangov and they ignored their highest interests and the class struggle. In this introduction P.Pouliopoulos placed the question of the Macedonian question on the first plane and from the burning peasant and refugee problem.

"The Macedonian question- he referred to- appears today for our party as a question which has an immediate influence in the political life in our country". "It is the basic issue of our country".

How could Pouliopoulos assert that a few thousand Bulgaro Macedonians were the centre of political action in our country?

How could he underrate the workers movement which was paying in blood the after-effects of the war? And the question of the Greek refugees which lived in the poor slums and were hungry. Alongside the peasant question which in this period was in an insurrectionary turmoil?

"The main issue is not to aid the self-determination of nations but that of the proletariat" (Lenin: On the National Question).

This view ignored by the defenders of the independence of 'Macedonia'. They believed that the national question would be the bomb which would destroy capitalism once and for all. Thus they underrated the struggle the struggle for social liberation with the result being, instead of overthrowing capitalism they destroyed the party!
"The position of the refugees – said P.Pouliopoulos - regarding the slogan of Macedonia will needs to studied carefully after analysing the statistics"!!! Pouliopoulos did not take into account that not one of the 750.000 refugees which based themselves in a new Macedonianthracian state!

Whilst Pouliopoulos would determine the position of the party with respect a careful study of the refugee situation and that the refugee situations would have to be broken off from their all-Greek structure and be embodied inside the "Macedonian" structure next to the armed fighters of EMEO. The party structures in Macedonia rebelled. They created a particular group especially organized. Nicolis, Tsiasopoulos and other close collaborators of Pouliopoulos attacked the followers of the Macedonian question.

How could Pouliopoulos have ignored the seismic reaction of the Party base in Macedonia with regards to the stupid Macedonian issue of self-determination?

It was true that Kordatos said that the refugees would go to fascism against the KKE if they were asked to become refugees in another state such as Macedonia one?

During this period during which Stalin declared that Chiang Kai Shek his friend and declared him a member of the Communist International ordered the Chinese CP. to enter the Bourgeois Kuomintang subdued is to the discipline of the Kuomintang and demanded it to block the peasant revolutionary and stop the creation of soviets which flourished everywhere so as to not come into conflict with Chiang and they viewed the revolution in China (1925-27) as bourgeois-democratic and not proletarian while in the spring of 1927 the communist took power in Shanghai for three months and they created soviets and nationalization.

In the end Chiang Kai Shek killed around 30.000 communists and sent thousands to prison. Whilst these events were coming to fruition in China, Stalin organized the same betrayal in Greece through his agent Manuilisky imposing the ridiculous national question:
To form an organisation of the Macedonian masses on the basis of the national question and to:

- Adapt the peasant demands of the Party with the analogy of the national peculiarities of Macedonia and Thrace.

- Adopt the United Front with the Revolutionary organizations.
- Form a common action with the Communist parties of Serbia and Bulgaria for the creation in Macedonia of a united national revolutionary organization or Party''.

According to this the program of the KKE was called to act from common here and now with the Serbia and Bulgarian Communist Parties one for a common Party! A clear Macedonian one. Let us forget the name Macedonia.

In Greece the KKE would have to be divided into two! The one would be Greek and the other Macedonian! The program of the KKE for the dictatorship of the proletariat, for soviets, for revolutionary internationalism would become second rate. The first task would be the organization of 'Macedonia' masses on the masses on the basis of the national-Macedonian issue and not the class struggle issues. The question as to whether it was proletarian was redundant.

L Karliaftis
1993

Archeio-Marxist Study Circle in 1924

THE NATIONAL QUESTION AND COMMUNISM ON THE MACEDONIAN QUESTION

It is possible to create a revolutionary movement in Greece without the struggle against nationalism in general and in particular on the Macedonian issue. The nationalism of the KKE not only aided the traitorous policy of class co-operation- Popular front. (The same is allied for the archeio with its provocative chauvinism on the Macedonian issue and its soft popular frontist policy). It aided its capitulation to the dictatorship, will manifest during the war with popular frontist positions on all the questions eg. On the national question, Dodecanese Cyprus.

We are lacking here the documents regarding the history of our theory and our policy on the national question in general. We are nothing from our memory a few things.

The discussions in German Social democracy (especially in austro-marxism, Bauers " National Question" and Kautsky's reply) was for general theory what defined a nation etc. Bauer considered criteria for the definition of a nation, Language and cultural elements for the common historical adventures. Common end: reform peacefully within the boundaries of the eventual conquests of national bourgeoisie.

The theory of Bolshevism once more placed on the basis of revolutionary Marxism on the question of nationalities of the Russian empire as Marx had first placed it on the Irish question. Lenin's discussions with the 'bandits' and with Rosa on the polish question enlightened its correct estimation and the tasks inside the era of imperialism and the world socialist revolution. Stalin in his brochure which supported opportunist views attacked as such by Lenin. Anyway we do not hold a precise account of this polemic which anyway holds a secondary importance for what is under discussion.

The bundists and all the opportunists inside Russian social democracy supported automarxists (minor nationalism and pacifism) views. This is the first tendency which was fought by the Russian Marxists Lenin, Trotsky. A second tendency was the mechanical concentration which occurred in the name of the economic socialist ideal of the future centralized economy to serve tsarism on the national question (in this direction did the anti-0stalinist polemic of Lenin turn on the Georgian question). The third view which was correctly attacked was Roza's: No national liberation can exist of the enslaved nationalities under capitalism and especially the polish nationality in our era. Thus: only socialistic revolutionary slogans to be raised, not national ones.

The policy of Bolshevism on the national question was developed at the 2nd and 3rd World Congress of the Communist International; with the thesis on the colonial movement, which is a national peasant question. Our principled positions are well known but we will remind with a few explanations.

1. Lenin replied before the war to Rosa: it's not strictly true that it is impossible to achieve independent state existence the enslaved peoples under capitalism before the

socialist revolution. As it occurred for Norway and thus could occur for Poland.

2. Naturally final and true national liberation can only be achieved with the socialist revolution. But it is a mistake to hold a minus political view towards the national revolutionary movements and to attempt to make it an element of the revolutionary movement for the overthrow of capitalist power in the world.

3. For the leadership of the national liberation movement (peasant majority of colonial peoples, backward or small minorities in Europe) today will be fought by the bourgeoisie and the newly born proletariat. The bourgeoisie even if it does defend in the beginning (India, China) finally and even during the course of the national liberating struggle will compromise with the oppressors or foreign imperialists. That's why our policy should be: Alongside the enslaved people for liberation until secession-but independent political position against the traitorous to the national-liberating cause bourgeoisie- for the proletarian power which on its own has full guarantee for the victory against the foreign occupier. A unity of struggle for the overthrow of national and social yoke. (Here Lenin and Trotsky attacked the opportunist tendencies bon the Indian Communist M.N.Roy at the congress of the C.I. especially the $2n^d$ and 3rd.).

4. The destructive results of the Stalinist policy in China (1925-27, 1936-40) have as its main source Stalinist opportunism on the motional-colonial question: abandonment of the independent position of the proletariat.

5. The possibility of the newly born proletariat of the oppressed nationality in the colonial and backward a small peoples to demand the leadership of the national liberating struggle is based

a) (The general character of the epoch,

b) The aid of the advanced proletariat in the metropolitan countries.,

6. The revolutionary proletariat of the oppressed nation defending the right of liberation of the oppressed nationality fulfils a fundamental principle:
7. a) for the internationalist education of the masses for the final secession from the influence of the ideology of the ruling class

b) For the victory of the socialist rebuilding of tomorrow. The English proletariat which cannot demand from now the national liberation of the Irish is not in a position to fight for its own social liberation from the English Capitalist power- said Marx the middle of the last century.

Amongst the exploited masses, proletarian and peasants and oppressed nationalities and the proletariat of the oppressed nation it is unavoidable that illusion of hatred and despair are cultivated and general alienation from their class brothers. An element of mass psychology which disallows the serious unity of all the oppressed in their struggle against the common and the social enemy, without disallowing their fraternization for socialistic rebuilding.

Alienation and distract cannot be fought against unless from now the proletariat and the peasantry of the oppressed nationality is truly and not in words for the liberation from now under the BOURGEOIS REGIME this proletariat is ready to fight with them for their national liberation until state secession, if that be its wish.

The internationalist spirit was given by bolshevism from the time of the tsar towards the countless nationalities of the Russian empire and thus gained their trust towards the new ruling class- in other words towards their voluntary federation and their brotherly cooperation for the socialist rebuilding. It is well known that the latter gave the greatest cultural autonomy ever known by a bourgeois or social democratic theoretician of the national question. The Stalinist authoritarianism abolishes this pre-condition today and prepares new dividing explosions creating a big danger for whatever has remained of the Conquests of October (Ukraine today).

On the Macedonian issue the different views, the historical and ethnological issues involved are aptly demonstrated by Lukas Karliaftis. Especially the immediate demands which are put forward at the end of the article which summarize our position very well. Their final slogans are generally abstract and as such do not have the essential characteristic of the communist slogans, its concrete forms and its immediate understanding from the wider masses.

1.   Liberation of the Macedonian nationality until state secession

---

2.   A Balkan Federation of Socialist Soviet Democracies. These must be our slogans generally. It's incorrect that the position of the KKE and the Archeio are 'bundist' or 'austromarxist'. These two parties the Archeio always the KKE from 1932 NEVER DEMANDED ONE DEMAND OF THE MACEDONIANS. THEY IGNORE CLEARLY THEIR EXISTENCE AND ASSERT THAT THE GREEK BOURGEOISIE SOLVED THE PROBLEM with the twin sided population transfer in Macedonian, in other words the Greek Bulgarian exchange and the Greek-Turkish exchange. It's on this issue that they are agents of Greek nationalism pure and simple. Never before has a Stalinist MP spoken about an essential question of the Macedonians in Parliament?

3.   Inside all the tragedies which constitute the so-called vanguard of Akronafplia the most tragic is for there to be Macedonians as followers of Stalinism.

In their criticism which comrade L. Karliaftis makes towards the old slogan of the KKE (1924-5) need explanations and additions so as to avoid mistakes which not only have historical importance. It's correct that the slogan:" United and Independent Macedonian and Thrace" of the 7th Balkan Congress and the emergency congress of the KKE in 1924 was unfounded.

1.   Thracian nationality doesn't exist. The mixture of Turks and Greeks (there was a very small minority there of Bulgarians) does not place the national question in that form there ('Thracian nation') – this is evident.

2.   This slogan places the Macedonian question on a geographical plane and not on a national one which it is. Geographically Macedonian is territory which does not create confusion amongst the Bulgarian 'autonomist' nationalists and those demanding the liberation of Macedonian nationality. This nationality is only concrete in only a small part of the geographical 'entity' called Macedonia. Here L.Karliaftis is good, revolutionary policy is not determined by statistics-borders as the ethnologists and 'socialist' lackeys of the Balkan bourgeoisie, but dynamic revolutionary and after the revolution leaves the determination of the free national boundaries in a true free union of interested brotherly peoples.

But confusion can create problems if slogans are presented in a wrong manner to the oppressed masses and can end up obstructing instead of aiding our international policy. They did truly obstruct them:

With the amazing ease the Greek proletariat accepted the new super chauvinist policy of the KKE which took over. What severe chaos was created inside the minds of all the militants and how this obstructed and will obstruct the internationalist education from the Party!

But the mistake of the slogans is not even Thrace 9 which was lacking from all the documents of the KKE even from the 1st December 1924 such was the force of realty) nor the 'un-geographical' boundaries of the Macedonian issue. Those slogans were clearly opportunist of the worst type. For those who do or have an opinion of the views of the first left oppositionists group inside the KKE and later "Spartans" on this important issue, let us add a few here:

After the first Bulgarian defeat (1923) and the second(1924) and after the great German defeat of 1923, the Stalinist bureaucracy which then started to develop and undermine the International (the period of Zinoviev-Stalinist adventurism of 1924-26) centred its European policy and the national insurrection (Raditch, Slovaks, Czechs, Ukrainians, Macedonians etc). The main spokesperson at the 5th Congress Manuilisky (1924) said:

The bombs we are placing for the victory of the in Europe are now: the national insurrections. Central slogan which overrode all else in the 5th Congress was the national issue.

Then the KKE was obliged to place the Macedonian issue at the centre of its work- as Dimitrov and Kolarov in Moscow- only thus would we win the Komitatsides in our ALLIANCE FOR THE OCCUPATION OF POWER IN Bulgaria. The KKE must be ready for every sacrifice for the Bulgarian revolution. As the opportunist leaders of the Bulgarian KKE destroyed the movement, they fell into the opportunist trap when they believed with the power of the proletariat and the peasants they didn't talk power, they would take it with the political alliance they signed in May 1924 in Vienna with Alexandrov and Protogerov. In six months alone that shady alliance collapsed proving the endless blindness of the Bulgarian party-Stalinist under construction leadership of Kolarov-Dimitrov. Alexandrov was murdered , the Protegerov and the Macedonian Komitatsides who once more played their bloodthirsty role against the workers and peasants communists of Bulgaria (slaughters after the Sweta-Nendelia putsch, April 1925) fell 9ijn turn victims to the 'centuries of friendship' of the Serbia and Bulgarian bourgeoisie.

The Macedonian movement as a separate revolutionary organization was termed illegal and inside Bulgaria. According to the logic of the policy of opportunism towards the Macedonian Komitate our slogan should not express an a priori principle with respect to the national Macedonian question but should ask for an independent Macedonian and Thrace. That is why when the extremist Zinovievite of the rising Stalinist bureaucracy was followed by opportunist bukharinist after its consumption of the Balkan movement, Batsuleskou vice-president of the International was sent to Greece to say suddenly…'retract the slogan' at the same time as the C.C. of the party needed during the court proceedings to save the public face of the party and of proletarian internationalism, The KKE thus sent to space the ridiculous order of Stalin and Manouilisky bomb was proved to be not at the foundations of European capitalism but of European Communism. Truly within a year all the national literature of 1924 had been transformed into the disastrous archives of the stalinised International.

At the 3rd Congress of the KKE (March 1927) the Stalinist representative of the C.I. Remele (after having slandered Trotskyism and the first oppositionist group in the KKE later ended up in the concentration camp in Turkestan and finally to the execution squad). Retracted essentially the slogan. But typically he supported it against our oppositionist group of typical reasons of internal consumption and pride of the bureaucracy, exploiting the general faith in the party towards the International of Lenin and the ignorance of the upcoming rise of the Russian oppositional movement.

1. Whoever refutes the existence of an unsolved until now national Macedonian question in Greek, Serbian, Macedonia is nothing but al lackey of the bourgeoisie.
2. Whoever refuted the historical liberationist movement of the Macedonians, they are uneducated and therefore they must learn the history of the movement and its national heroes or is a lackey of one of the three oppressed bourgeoisie.
3. This movement until now has been drowned in blood and betrayal or has suffered a destructive for the interests of the Macedonian workers and peasants exploitation from the (Bulgarian primarily) Balkan bourgeoisie.
4. This movement can find a new development under favourable new historical conditions – social, economic (fierce exploitation of the Macedonian

masses from the occupying national bourgeoisie, questions of land ownership etc.) political 9 internal crisis on the Balkan states, war) and cultural conditions.

5. Whoever refutes this possibility is either blind or a lackey of those who implement population transfers against the Macedonian peoples.

6. Communists do not undertake to 'create' national movements there where they do not exist. They support such movements where they manifest themselves.

7. The communists in front of a defeated or betrayed national liberation movement or in front of nationalist and population transfers of their national bourgeoisie do not close their eyes and do not become followers of the final event. We will not refute the existence of national oppression of one nationality and its desire (which exists in the heart and mind of every Macedonian worker) to get rid one day the national yoke. The communists make their own these liberationist desires of the Macedonian people and declare openly their desire for self-determination until state secession if that be their wish. They defend every day immediate and national demand, economic, political and cultural and thus prepare tomorrow's revolutionary alliance of the social revolutionary movement of the proletariat with the national revolutionary

movement of the Macedonians against the common enemy, the Balkan Bourgeoisie.

**Akronafplia,
May 1940**

Pandelis Pouliopoulos

PART D

APPENDIX A:
THE ARCHEIO-MARXIST MOVEMENT 1923-30

Any historical analysis of the Archeio-Marxist movement will show that an alternative existed to the stalinist degeneration of the KKE . How does one explain the existence of the organisation of the similar size, which grew parallel and independent of the KKE and the CI in the 1920's yet not allied with Stalin? Above all what is its significance when judged with KKE throughout the 1920's?

Was the Archeio-Marxist movement one "whose 'activity' of its few followers manifested itself with murderous attempts and terrorist acts against the communists"(1) parallely serving the interests of the Greek bourgeoisie? Here for example is what the rising stalinist bureaucracy in the KKE wrote in 1927:

"The basic distinction which divides the Archeio Marxists from the KKE and the CI is based on the fact thee Archeio-Marxists start from a different class basis hostile towards the interests of the proletariat and the other oppressed masses.": This basic distinction is manifested in the organisational principles and tactics of the Archeio-Marxists, principles and tactics which have nothing in common with the principles and tactics of the world communist movement… The Archeio-Marxists with its hostile attacks against the party, with the dissolution of the trade unions which they are organising alongside the treacherous distortion of marxist-leninist theory, is aiding not negatively or indirectly but the bourgeoisie directly"(2)

The publication of the "Archives of Marxism" on Mayday 1923 and the expulsion of F. Tzoulatis in 1924 occurred at a decisive turning point in the international communist movement. Tzoulatis was expelled under the pretext that he was "teaching pseudo-marxism and calling their sectarian underground activity 'illegal action' but in essence it is liquidating and degenerating activity…" (3)

Haitas expulsion of Tzoulatis and later of Pouliopoulos was the first in a long series of expulsions against people who were to ally themselves with Trotsky.

1923 is the year when the left opposition was born in the USSR the German revolution was crushed and thermidorean reaction made its appearance signalling the bureaucratic degenerations of the USSR the CPSU and the CI. The year 1923-4 can be taken as a turning point in the development of the struggle for a revolutionary party in Greece.

The previous ideological struggles of the period 1918-23 of the communists left Tzoulatis –Ligdopoulos against the right-wing reformist leadership of the SEKE was undoubtedly part of a broader international phenomenon: the crisis of development of the CI through which under Lenin and Trotsky's leadership the international communist vanguard was educated and selected. The ideological struggles after 1924 had to deal with a totally different crisis inside the CI: the crisis provoked by the defeat of the European revolution and the bureaucratic degeneration of the UISSR and the CI. The changes in the international arena and the rise of stalinism confront the Greek labour movement, especially after the Asia=minor expedition with the most thorough transformations of its history. Stalinism was able to gain roots inside the immature and nascent workers movement which had still not overcome the level of typically accepting Lenin's 21 conditions of entry into the CI in 1920.

At the start of 1925 the 2nd Congress of the Archeio-Marxists occurred and the mainly discussed the finances of the journal. But parallely a discussion emerged concerning a New International as the CI and Trotsky had analysed was degenerating fast. But the situation both on a national, as well as an international scale did not allow and the Archeio-Marxists quite correctly did not openly call for a new party or a new international. They considered themselves a faction of the CI and their devotion to the principles of the Russian Revolution made them the number one enemies of nascent Greek stalinism. The leadership of Sargologou-Stavrides in the KKE handed over sellers of the Archeio's journal to the police. The leadership Apostolides-Maximos-Kordatos-Maximos called "fascist group". The journal quite succinctly replied: "We have already published many of the classic works of Marxist… We are obliged to protest a sycophancy published in "Rizospastis" with which the journal, "Archives of Marxism" are termed a 'fascist organ'. We protest because the greatest persecution against the distribution of Marxist literature in our country is occurring by people who say they are working for the progress of the movement". (4)

No serious student of history can doubt that the source of all these slanders against the first Greek Trotskyists and generally all oppositionists were be found in Moscow.

At the start of the 1926 Tzoulatis and Giotopoulos took over the leadership of the Archeio-Marxists. The logo of their journal noted " Prota morfosi istera Drasi"(Education first then Activity). And many criticised the Archeio-Marxists that they were simply a theoretical discussion club and not politically active in the labour movement. These criticisms are valid in its initial period of formation. They lacked an independent political newspaper, like the KKE's "Rizospastis", but from 1925 onwards serious attention and a turn towards the labour movement were undertaken. Just a few examples of the ARCHEIO-Marxists penetration of the labour movement are described in C. Castritis (L. Karliaftis) account. (5)

1. General strike in Agrinio led by archeio marxists in 1926. For one month the whole of Agrinio with elected strike committees workers militiants and no scabs held out against Pangalos dictatorship. With the outbreak of the strike the KKE sent Tsatsakos from Athens with the order of ending the strike. But the members of the KKE in Argini refused to obey such a strike breaking decision. A reporter of "Rizospastis" characteristically wrote " for the first time such a strike occurs without scabs and during Pangalos' dictatorship' It should be written in golden words for history".(6) Eventually the strikers won achieving the rise they were demanding and Pangalos fell.

2. Bakers strike in Athens in 1927. The leadership of the bakers union is won by the Archeio-Marxists Silas and Sakkos. After conflict with the police the

strike is victorious and the bakers gain a wage increase and the right to a pension scheme.

3. Shoemakers strike in Athens in 1928 led by the Archeio-Marxists which held out for fifty days. It failed abysmally in its demands after the police crushed it and imprisoned its leaders.

4. In Piraeus thousands of seafarers, dockers and industrial workers existed. The Archeio-Marxists by 1928 were probably more stronger than the KKE. P. Pouliopoulos was to note that, "the greatest centre of the industrial proletariat in our country Piraeus, continues to be inaccessible for the Party. Another separatist organisation functions there, which makes gains among factory workers, distributes Leninists-Marxists works, holds general meetings on communist theory and in the name of communism fights the party and asks for its liquidation./ In which other country does a similar phenomenon exist? (7)

5. Student's riots shake Athens in 1929. Over 3.500 students go on strike. Hundreds are arrested and beaten by the police in Athens. The Archeio-Marxists had a strong presence in the students who after going on a hunger strike gain a partial satisfaction of their demands.

The divisions and physical battles between the stalinist KKE and the Archeio-Marxist trotskyists reached violent proportions when two militants were murdered by the KKE.

Georgopapadatoas a baker by profession was stabbed by a gang led by N.Zachariades in 1927 and Ladas, a shoemaker suffered the same fate in 1928. Characteristic of Stalinisms gangsterous policies is a leaflet published by the Kavalas branch of the KKE which stated the following: "Comrades the Archeio-Marxists are the worst kind of agents of the police. No toleration towards them is necessary. Kick them out of the factories. Hit them wherever you see them. Hit them in the tobacco factories if you find them etc."

By 1930 contacts were made Trotsky's Left Opposition and the Archeio-Marxists become an official section of the ILO. Below are excerpts of a report on the state of the Left Opposition in Greece:
The Archeio-Marxists despite the fact that they remained outside the CI control are inspired in all their activity by the ideas of the Russian Revolution. The fact that they maintained their independence from 1923-4 influenced favourably the development of the Archeio-Marxists by the fact that they were guarded against the poison of Lenin's falsifiers, the leaders of the stalinist fashion. From 1923 the Archeio-Marxists start to be interested in the struggle of the Left Opposition in the USSR. Consequently they study in their ranks and accept without preconditions the criticisms of the Russian Opposition concerning the German Revolution of 1923, the defeat of the Chinese Revolution, The Anglo-Russian Committee and all the questions which deal with Soviet Russia. They translate into Greek the works of cde. Trotsky making them known

to broad layers of revolutionary workers. This work of assimilating the ideas of the ILO occurs parallel with the penetration of trade-union organisations and the economic struggles of the working class… the "Archives of Marxism" socialist parties which functioned under illegality… the branches number more than 1500 comrades. They have an influence inside trade unions which number more than 20.000 members. The leaderships in the unions of building workers, shoemakers, tobacco workers, bakery workers, woodworkers, steelworkers, and other sectors of the industry and public services are led these comrades. They publish trade union papers which are read by more than 7,000 workers. The leadership of the union for Disabled, Widows and Orphans of War, with 14.000 members is also under influence of our comrades…"(9)

The activity of the Archeio-Marxists for as long as it lasted was in the best traditions of communism. They remained committed to the organizational principles of Leninism, they were the first in Greece to publish and educate workers around the classic works of Marxism, they defended the concept of Soviet Democracy as opposed to the KKE's Popular Democracy and they struggled against the class collaborationist policies of the KKE (its relations with Plastiras, Pangalos, Patricios, Kondilis, Demertsis). After 1930 the Archeio- Marxists became the largest official section of the ILO and in recognising their importance Trotsky was to write:
"The Organization of Archeio-Marxists has its roots in the special conditions of Greece and until Three years ago developed separately and independently from the Left Opposition. But as it has occurred many times in history at

a certain point our paths met. Will it last? For how long? I think it will last and forever. Due to its militant proletarian composition the Organization of Archeio-Marxists has proved itself most able to assimilate and implement politically the Ideas of the Left Opposition than certain other old sections. The Greek section of Bolshevik-Leninists can maintain its organisation on the path it has chosen, all the more stably if it is able to give to its young proletarian cadres a serious theoretical education". (10)

1.Kommunismos-Communism Periodical
2.Archeion Marxismou – Archives of Marxism
3.Pali ton Taxeon-Paper 'Class Struggle' in the 1930's

APPENDIX B:
THE SPARTAKOS: OPPOSITION IN THE KKE

It is impossible to understand the political role of the "Spartakos" Opposition without starting from the international frame work which determined it.

Under the pressure of imperialism the first workers state which was established in a peasant country (USSR) started to develop conservative bureaucracy. The troika Zinoviev-Kamenev-Stalin which after Lenin's death provisionally became in change of the CPSU and the CI adapted to these pressures and the rising bureaucracy. At the 5th Congress of the CI which Pouliopoulos attended, the significance of the German defeat (1923) was concealed and ultra-left illusions for immediately revolutionary explosions were projected. But as Trotsky showed behind the ultra-left cover a right wing turn would follow.

So as to establish a pseudo leftwing policy a whole series of left-wing leaderships were established in the CP's/ AS Trotsky noted all the CP's found themselves " trapped amongst the directives of the 5th Congress on the one hand and political reality on the other".(1)

This contradiction provoked disasters. In Bulgaria it led to individual terrorism. In Estonia to a failed communist coup. In Greece it had two direct and disastrous results. Firstly in the opportunist projection of the slogan for an "Independent Macedonia and Thrace" resulting in a forthcoming workers and peasant's revolution in Bulgaria and the Balkans as Manuilinsky had proclaimed. Secondly the revolution never came; instead we had a serious conflict inside the KKE, confusion among its members and the masses coupled with violent persecutions from the class enemy. Despite the fact that Pouliopoulos disagreed with the slogan he heroically defended the party when placed on trial.

The 5th congress of the C.I. orientated the CP's towards the apparent 'revolutionary' capabilities of non-proletarian and anti-proletarian forces like the peasant parties of Randich and Lafollette's, Chiang-Kai-Shek or Pilsudski. With this orientation in mind the KKE turns towards 'red officers' of the Greek bourgeois army, even towards the dictator Pangalos.

Pouliopoulos fought to correct this course but the Stalinist Zachariades-Haitas-Eftihiades blocked him. The zinovievite-stalinist phase of the CI did not take long in ending. Stalin's bureaucracy came into conflict with Zinoviev who was turning towards Trotsky. The stalinists using administrative methods overturned all the left-wing leaderships established by Zinoviev's leadership in the 5ty congress of the CI (e.g. the Trent group in France, Fischer-Maslow in Germany, Pouliopoulos in Greece etc).

Pouliopoulos undertook the struggle against the stalinist degeneration of the KKE by publishing the document 'Neo Xekinima' (New Start) in June 1927. Its basic ideas are summed up in the following way:
'QA loss in the quantitative level of the members. Petty bourgeois and anti-proletarian psychology. Many lumpen proletariat who are members. An atmosphere of corruption and gossip. Adventurism.'

"We are not even today an attempt at a vanguard. Blind action in the dark and worthless noise-that's what our activity comprises of...

"The KKE will never become serious if it does not rally to its ranks a chosen number of proletarians and intellectuals. Such was the starting point of all the CP's and above all the Russian..."(2)

During the period of the 'bolshevisation' the KKE undertook to rally to its ranks 5000 new members. Anyone could join and this led to the lowering of the political level of the whole party and at the same time exposing in to the real danger of police agents. Pouliopoulos criticisms lead to the expulsion of around 300 people. The party became dived into two. A minority inside the politburo around Maximos,

Sklavos, Hainoglou, defended Pouliopoulos and Giatsopoulos, but were soon expelled themselves.
The new leaders of the CI undertook a slanderous campaign against Pouliopoulos and his comrades. Their main criticism was that he had apparently asserted that the KKE should be liquidated. This charge had previously been fabricated by Bukharin against Trotsky to show that Trotsky was apparently for a new party, against the USSR and therefore a 'capitulator'.

Smeral then wrote in Pravda:
'The Struggle Against the Capitulationist Right-wing in the KKE'.
'The Greek CP was forced to expel from its ranks Pouliopoulos who is an intellectual and not from proletarian origins. He joined the Party in 1922 as a leader

of the veterans of War…" After 3 months (actually 2 years) he becomes secretary of the KKE. He spends two years in jail. By autumn 1926 an impression is created of the illegal Party. The 3rd congress of the KKE with the support of the CI condemned Pouliopoulos' wrong principles. It isolated him from the party but did not take away the possibility of allowing him to return to the Leninist line inside the ranks of the Party. But Pouliopoulos became an extreme right-wing capitulator. Petty bourgeois anarchic intellectual individualism won him over, which in essence is foreign towards proletarian ideology…

"In the last two months the capitulationist group in Greece has opted for the terminology and tactics of the factionalist struggle of the Opposition in The CPSU.
"In "Neo Xekinima" he writes that the official organ of the party is not the organ of the whole Party. The Party is Led by a faction.

"In criticising our criticisms he declares solidarity with the Opposition in the USSR. We are he asserts 'against the theory of socialism in one country, we consider it anti-Leninist, anti-Marxist'.
"After period of a year our patience ended and he was expelled. Pouliopoulos will soon end up where the logic of events has led Ruth Fischer and Souvarine and lose all connection with the international workers movement". (3)
The "Spartakos" opposition in 1927 did not have a clear idea of the international roots of the conflict. In an article by Pouliopoulos titled "Problems of the Communist Opposition in Greece" the root causes of all disagreements

is a misunderstanding of the 'period which the communist and workers movement is experiencing in Greece"(4) Pouliopoulos defended the theory of the oppositionist Sklavos which was termed the 'theory of the two sides'. According to this the tasks of the KKE were twofold: On the one hand they are the revolutionary tasks of a leninist party fighting for the establishment of a workers and peasants government, on the other they are the tasks of educating the workers like social democracy did in the West.

The stalinists criticised Sklavos as being a reformist and he replied that he was not trying to combine reformism with communism but the dialectically relate the tasks of two different periods inside current Greek reality.

A common view point against stalinists by both oppositionists groups (Sklavos-Maximos and Pouliopoulos-Giatsopoulos) who made up the "Spartakos" Opposition was their attempt to see how the laws of combined and uneven development manifested themselves in Greece. They attempted to overcome not only the reformist theory of stages, but also the schematic view which levelled out and removed the peculiarities of the Greek socioeconomic model.

This brought the "Spartakos" Opposition close to the Left Opposition. They defended in 1927 with declarations Trotsky and the Left Opposition whom were being persecuted. They condemned the opportunist politics of Stalin-Bukharin on the question of Anglo-Russian Committee, the defeat of the Chinese Revolution and the problems of economic development in the USSR.

In other words on the main issues which divided Stalin and Trotsky, the Spartakos group supported Trotsky. But on one question which was decisive the Spartakos group did not take a clear stand: the question of permanent revolution.

Someone can negate the theory of socialism in one country (as "Spartakos" did) without accepting its only consistent alternative, the theory of permanent revolution. The experience of Zinoviev and his supporters in the United Opposition (1926-7) shows this.

The zinovievites were against an adaption to the Kulaks, Nepmen etc, who were being strengthened under the umbrella of the stalinism dogma of 'socialism in one country' but did they not accept the theory of permanent revolution- this being one of the basic reasons for their eventual capitulation. Without accepting the theory of permanent revolution an opposition movement could not be described as trotskyist much it agreed on other points. From this point of view the declarations of the "Spartakos" Opposition were not qualitatively different from parallel oppositionist groups in the same period in other sections of the CI.

In 1928 a law passed in the Greek Parliament whereby not only were 'subversive' actions persecuted but the ideas of communism as well. The "Spartakos groups was severally repressed and most of its members languished in prison. A split occurred in the group near the end of 1929 among Pouliopoulos' and Sklavos' factions leading to an organizational disarray. Its only in 1930 that "Spartakos" reappeared as a periodical after having ceased publication in April 1928. Political differences with the Archeio-Marxists meant that the "Spartakos" group was not officially recognised in 1930 by Trotsky. Its subsequent evolution alongside the London Bureau in the early 1930'as was only halted after Pouliopoulos orientated himself irrevocably towards Trotsky's Fourth International, under whose banner he has executed by Italian fascists at Nezero concentration camp in 1943.

Greek Trotskyists imprisoned in the 1930's

Appendix C:
Michel Raptis: From Archeio-Marxism to Fractionism.
The creation of the KEO (Communist Unity Group)

The first political steps of Michel Raptis (later to be known as Pablo and leader of the Fourth International after Trotsky's death) is when he joins the Archeio group and advances alongside other members of this after a great period of confusion and research to the creation of the KEO.

Pablo writes in his autobiography characteristically "Fractionism is organised in 1931 in the KEO group and it publishes the 'Bulletin' to which I write anonymously with the pseudonym Spiros. There I first make my political steps..."1.

For an understanding of the political positions and the political presentation of the KEO I used the official organ called the 'Bulletin' which was carried with the monthly theoretical organ of the Communist Unity Group (Left Opposition). In Rizospastis of that era one can see reports of the leading cadres of the organisation M. Soula. The main bulk of the forces of the Left Opposition in Greece did not come from the forces which politically originated from the KKE but from the Archeio-Marxists.

Under pressure of the members who thirsted for revolutionary action this organisation turns towards mass activity in particular trade union circles where its members developed its activity without any serious help from the leadership of the organisation, which whilst asking for theoretical understanding didn't actually have it. This event, the poverty of theory for the movement as a whole, of which the Archeio was only a small component led to divisions within the organisation.

Soulas refers to these problems in his discussion with the leader of the organisation Giotopoulos:
"He never told me to read a book or whether he read a book he never made any remarks about it. He never made any remarks regarding daily work or gave any advice. Once as a representative of the bakers in their annual Congress in 1928 I asked my opinion of the delegation and he replied in a simple sentence "swear at them".

Raptis himself refers to Archeio-Marxism as having "stayed there for a short period of time. As to the extent that my knowledge in Marxism advanced and my experience increased as to the way this organisation functioned and acted, I found that I had a big contradiction between theory and practice, principles and education..."3.

It is characteristic that the memories of M. Soulas about the political isolation by the organisation of those it considered necessary.

According to M.Soulas in a period when he was an active trade-unionist he received the following instructions from the leader of the organisation Giotopoulos (beginning of 1929) "You will call him and tell him he will be taken out of the organisation due to his dodgy past once and for all. I carried out his wishes but I hadn't been convinced that it was a justified act. The victim, I remember felt very uneasy about his isolation... But he added that he would never act against the organisation"4.

A small time later M. Soulas was also found outside the organisation in a similar fashion. These expulsions did not automatically lead to a political situation. Discussion became tiresome.

Soulas himself preferred to isolate himself from Athens on an island for a brief period of time. Despite the fact that the movement had started to form itself in the period when the representatives of the International Left Opposition had come to Greece, the so-called fractionists never came into contact with them to inform them.

The movement spreads to the organisations in Athens-Piraeus-Thessaloniki- and Agrinio which was one of the most basic organisations.

In June 1931 it circulates the 'Bulletin' (Monthly theoretical organ of the KEO (Left Opposition) and the speeches and discussions of the first National Conference. In this journal there is an extensive referral to the causes of the conflict with Archeio-Marxism.

In a basic article of the group with the title our positions we see the following estimations… "Our group which appears today with the 'Bulletin' constitutes all the cdes. Of the 'fractionists' of Archeio-Marxism all the cdes. Who participated in a review of past struggles and towards a revolutionary orientation for the current problems of the movement"… Whilst for Archeio-Marxism it is noted that it is a fierce faction of conspirators which chose and enriched its structures with trusted, dedicated young revolutionary communists it developed to an extent an internal regime of 'monolithism' which in reality meant ignorance to all, wooden discipline which meant blind subservience to the unmistakeable secret principle and 'trust' translated to close personal relationship".

It must be added that the conflict was imposed as a 'reaction to a degenerated organisational regime". For the organisational presence of the group it must be underlined that the necessity of the policy of autonomy must be preserved as neither the KKE nor the Archeio reflects the demands of the revolutionary struggle. Whilst we ask for the cooperation of all the forces of the opposition into a united organism"…5

The KEO's Stance on the KKE

A basic element of the political differentiation of the newly formed organisation from the Archeio is the policy which must be followed. The KKE in this period is in a deep political and organisational crisis. The policy of 'social fascism' found it in total conflict with all the tendencies and groups of the workers movement. As characteristically noted by A. Elefantis, "the KKE creates a divisive line amongst this and the rest of the political world and declares who isn't with us is a fascist"…6

In the trade-union movement the situation is very difficult. After the 4th Congress of GSEE (May 1928) where we have the expulsion of trade-unionists, and the expulsion of unions the leadership of the KKE advances to create the Revolutionary GSEE.

At the founding congress of the R.GSEE (February 1929) members of the Archeio and Spartakos make criticisms of the leadership of the GSEE. The very next day a proposal by Theos' to ban all the Archeios from the unions creates mass hysteria from the Archeios who were in and out of the theatre and this led to a terrible conflict where they fought with guns, knives, sticks etc. Members of both camps suffered immensely and many were arrested after the police intervened. (7)

The chasm which divided the members of both organisations had been transformed into blind hatred. In the union movement, due to the split of GSEE and the policy of social-fascism which followed the KKE, a small percentage of workers took part in the unions.

The KEO despite the intense conflict with the forces of the KKE emphasises its differentiated positions from those of Archeio-Marxism,
"The KKE and the political programme it represents, the international organs it belongs to and especially its history and methods of struggle is the organ of revolutionary struggle for the overthrow of the existing politico-social regime and the representative of the communist movement in our country"...(8)

Its political line is judged to be wrong. Its organisation declares it will carry out opposition in the framework of the International Left Opposition. As it is cleared ... "it means with this total organisational independence and initiative in all the points where its forces allow and support for the KKE in all the cases as a different position will in reality mean a split of the communist struggle…"(9)

A little later the KEO asks from the Politburo of the KKE "to stand on the shoulders of the revolutionary principles of leninism and to not refuse the right as revolutionary workers which we are, to fight inside the party for the revolution and Communism". Whilst parallely it is underlined that we belong to the ILO "cannot refuse us this right, as the ILO aims towards the re-birth of these parties"(10)

The leadership of the KKE through 3 articles of 'Rizospastis' (14,15, 16 September 1931) negates the demand of the members of the organisation. Its response is contained in the 3rd volume of the official articles of the KKE. 11 Here an extended presentation appears of the conflict of 'Leninism-Trotskyism' according to the stalinist presentation, refuting the demand of the members of the KEO for their entrance into the Party as they are near the ILO.

The KKE condemns the leadership of the KEO as, "attempting to continue its counterrevolutionary work, bargaining behind our backs with counterrevolutionary leaders, capitulationists, who were thrown out of the party, these frightened petty bourgeois as they refuted the necessity of the Party in today's period and they wanted to dissolve it"… As well as stating "they have a political line which wants to utilise the fact that because they weren't accepted as a faction in the Party, so as to justify the after the event struggle against the Party, the concentration outside the lines of the Party of a second counterrevolutionary party".

Finally the members of the KEO are called to renounce trotskyism and the organisation of factionists and enter the Party. The members of the KEO have this to say to the leadership of the KKE.

"Waiting for a time the Politburo maintains outside the organisational framework of the KKE and we will show more with the daily activity that we have inside the working masses our dedication to its political programme to broaden its bases, to stabilise its influence and to develop permanently inside its lines its influence as a real conscious members of its left flank" (12)

The members of the KEO during the electoral activity were on the side of the KKE. Very few were the members of the organisation which entered the KKE. It was mainly the members who had been murdered for the murder of the policeman Giftodimopoulos.

Their participation in the union movement.
The creation of KEO transformed the balance of forces where the Archeio had the overwhelming majority (bakers, shoemakers, confectionary etc.) The members of the KEO despite their criticisms which they made on the RGSEE, as the KKE was unable to increase the class organisation which it created and to minimise the reactionary spirit of the close dependence of the professional organisations on the Party"13 their main focus point are the forces of the Archeio-Marxists in the union movement.

Rizospastis refers to one of these union conferences, that of the bakers. "Yesterday in the meeting hall San Zousin we had the conference of bakers where 100 took part. In the beginning the arch-fascist Kavalieros spoke, who developed the programme of 'action' of the leadership, then the factionist Soulas, who then stated the line of Archeio is traitorous and proposed the entrance of the union into the Union of Food Supplies"14

On the unionist activity of the KEO its bulletin writes "The activity of the factions of our group in the centre of Thessaloniki had as a result the more large unions of the Pan-Worker Alliance (this divisive Archeio-Marxist block) (tailors, building-workers, printers, shoemakers) to become part of the Workers Centre in Thessaloniki after they have gotten rid of their Archeio-Marxist leaders."(15)

The intense appearance in the union movement is also made due to the writing in the Bulletin by Apostolides ex-secretary of the KKE and a leading cadre of the Union of Press workers. Apostolides writes about the very small organisational influence of the left forces on the working class and proposes the "creation of left factions in every professional organisation where full democracy can exist"16 the aim is to surpass the division and separate unions which characterise the strength of the unions.

Apostolides himself believed that the KEO constituted an attempt by the masses in "defence of a serious attempt to overcome divisions for unification and renewal"17
In a series of unions the members of the KEO achieve a serious number of votes.

Rizospastis for instance refers to the elections of the shoemakers of Piraeus that out of 210 which voted "the cdes which constituted the candidates of the revolutionary slate got 143 votes, the factionists got 71 and the archeio-fascists 53"18. Whilst the Bulletin in a response from Thessaloniki on the elections of the tailors refers to the fact that out of the 306 that voted the stalinist faction got 135, the Unity (KEO) faction 71, the Archeio 56 and Spartakos 44"(19)

Political Attacks

The political line of the Keo received attacks from all the streams of the Left. So much the KKE, as well as Archeio and the Spartakos organisation, which the KEO confronted with a positive way criticised it for its political line. A basic supporter of the line of the organisation from the lines of its Bulletin was M. Raptis who went under the name of Speros. In an article of his with the title 'A few thoughts on the history of composition of the group and its development" it underlines the course of its creation. "The period up until 'factionalism' inside the Archeio-Marxist organisations is characterised with a lack of a clear communist view with regards to the problems of the movement in our country and the non-existence of any ideological conflict, a low educational level and a weakness of the actualisation of mass revolutionary action"… He goes on to characterise the beginning of factionalism as an "unclear confused and disorienting conflict within the ranks of the Archeio-Marxist circles, which the internal weaknesses provoked as well as the objective conditions of a left turn and activity of the revolutionary movement"… Slowly but surely the…

"Situation clears continuously and the internal antagonisms are clarified in concrete elements". For M. Raptis the organisation … only then "can continue its task if parallely with its theoretical work, continues into a militant activity inside the hard battles which the proletariat of our country carries out"… (20)

The political support of the forces of the KKE in the union movement creates as it appears problems in the organisation and the correctness of these choices. In an article of M. Raptis in November 1931 it attempts to support the validity of these choices. According to M. Raptis "inside the masses our propaganda and our activity, must appear that it doesn't come from an organism separate from the Party, but from members of the Party which is the only general staff of the oppressed of this country"… He believes that the criticism levelled against KEO by the Archeio that they have become a tail-end of the Party is wrong.

He notes that if "today inside the Party a friendly audience exists towards the views of our group this is due to the fact that we had the courage to cut off every relation with our Archeio-Marxist past and on the other hand because our stance is everywhere aided so as to explain our views without preconditions, phraseology and empathy. Archeio-Marxism today widens the chasm amongst the members of the party and the ideas of the Opposition" The article concludes "All the revolutionaries inside the one and only KKE" (21)

The political orientation of KEO as a Left Opposition to the KKE makes it come close to its political decisions of

Spartakos. They start discussions for the common course of these organisations. But Pouliopoulos criticises KEO in a very severe manner, so much that a lot of what he says becomes extreme. In the end a committee is created which looks at the possibility of integrating both groups and the creation of a Congress which will finally resolve the situation. (22)

KEO survives for a brief period of time. A section of its members goes towards Spartakos, whose views are aired in the last copy of the Bulletin (May 1932). Another section creates alongside Stinas the LAKKE (Leninist Opposition to the KKE). A few of its members go and join the KKE. Clearly KEO was in a political crisis as it failed to maintain a plausible independent position from all the other political groupings.

Characteristically there was a letter of A. Dervisoglou in Neos Rizospastis who analysing the course of Archeio-Marxism makes bold statements against his ex-comrades. For the time of his presence in KEO he states nothing else happened but endless discussion and conflicts which led to a small part of its members to drop out altogether another to Spartakos and another to LAKKE. Clearly KEO was in a political crisis as it failed to maintain a plausible independent position from all the other political groupings.

Most of the issues confronting the KEO were those that confronted all the oppositional groupings from the KKE or the Archeio. In what manner and in what way could they change the policy of stalinism. In or out of the KKE the dilemma was the same. KEO attempted for a brief period of time to steer clear of all groupings but the weakness of its cadre, the weight of history and the poverty of its theory meant that it would eventually split and disintegrate. This doesn't imply that the same processes didn't happen to all the other groupings, but at that particular juncture in history KEO proved to be more brittle and unable to withstand the 'civil war' between the KKE and the Archeio which basically characterised the conflicts of that era.

Lukas Karliaftis in 2004 giving a Speech about Pouliopoulos at the Workers Centre in Thebes, Evia where Pouliopoulos was born

PART E
GREEK TROTSKYISM UNDER TRIPLE REPRESSION

1. The Founding Conference of the EOKDE and the Group's Activities

In spite of intense repression, arrests and unprecedented terror, and in addition to the fact that the finest members of the Trotskyist movement were already imprisoned in the concentration camps of the Metaxas dictatorship, the Trotskyists organised the founding conference of the United Organisation of the Communist Internationalists of Greece (EOKDE) in February 1937. The OKDE and the *New Course* groups, both having roots in the period of the Russian Revolution and the birth of Bolshevism and Trotskyism in Greece, united at this conference.

The establishment of the EOKDE was the result of the close cooperation and ideological discussion between the two tendencies throughout 1936. It played a genuinely revolutionary role during this period and through the magnificent revolt in Thessalonica. An unbreakable unity was forged, and in February 1937 a Trotskyist organisation was founded which would work within Trotsky's orientation for the building of the Fourth International. The circumstances in which this necessary and hopeful unification took place were harsh in the extreme. We could thus go so far as to call it an historical event.

The unity conference took place in February 1937 in a canyon in the Pentelis Mountains in Attica. It lasted one day and was attended by around 15 comrades, all of whom were well-known and had played a significant role in the history of the workers' movement. The prisoners in Acronauplia and the other concentration camps were not, of course, represented. In his closing speech, L Vourzoukis noted that there were more participants from the *New Course*. The new Central Committee comprised Pantelis Pouliopoulos, who became the leader of the united organisation, Michel Raptis and G Vryhoropoulos from the OKDE, and L Vourzoukis, K Anastasiadis and G Tamtakos from the *New Course*. Other participants included Nontas Giannakos, Lilis, M Kondilidis, Katsaprokos .Comrades who were still in jail under 12-month sentences that were renewed indefinitely were not eligible for the new Central Committee.

The conference resolution emphasised that the dictatorship in Greece showed that the bourgeoisie was obliged to construct a strong state apparatus that could deal with national divisions which had exploded in the rebellion in Thessalonica in May 1936, the workers' movement, and with any problems posed by the huge requirements of resources for the forthcoming world war:
'The dictatorship became inevitable as a result of the mounting anger of the masses, which was manifested in several long and revolutionary struggles all over the country, which, in the face of the worsening world economic crisis, combined with the revolutionary uprising of the Spanish Civil War, and the imminent threat of a new imperialist war, could be transformed into a generalised revolutionary storm.'

The conference stated that the main obstacle to the advance of the workers' movement was the Communist Party (KKE), which had led the workers' struggles to disaster, and, therefore, had helped Metaxas to impose his dictatorship. This party and its Popular Front policy bore the main responsibility for the ease with which the bourgeoisie imposed its dictatorship. It had covered up the aims of the bourgeois parties instead of exposing them, and it had helped them to concede full control of the army to the king, thus helping Metaxas to take power. Even then it still did not place a revolutionary perspective before the masses, but merely called for the replacement of the dictatorship by a bourgeois parliamentary government. It was necessary to wage a relentless, all-out struggle against this party, with the perspective of uniting all revolutionary forces in a new internationalist party, under the banner of the Fourth International.

Unity between the OKDE and the *New Course* took place, even though pre-conference discussions had not been fully concluded, and some points of difference had not been satisfactorily clarified. Nonetheless, unity was as necessary as it was constructive. Yes, historical, we might say. As the Trotskyists were united and armed both politically and theoretically, and strove for the formation of the Fourth International, they were therefore the only tendency prepared to face the coming approaching war in a Leninist manner. The political orientation of the conference was confirmed in a resolution of June 1937, which called: 'For an independent revolutionary struggle for the establishment of a workers' and peasants' government. That is the direction of the struggles of this period. Only thus will the workers be saved from the destruction and horror of the war.'

And continued by demanding:
'A United Front for the overthrow of the royal dictatorship in Greece, for support for the immediate political and economic demands of the workers, and for the rapid preparation for the rule of the workers and peasants.'

For us the approaching war was imperialist as far as the major powers were concerned, with the exception of the Soviet Union:
'The war does not cease to be imperialist because frauds and middle class philistines bandy around sugared slogans. War is an extension of the policies of finance capital. It is important to recognise which class makes the war. As Lenin said, the war is imperialist so long as it is carried out by the bourgeoisie with the aim of robbery. There is no greater fraud than the Stalinist and Social Democratic propaganda about it being an anti-Fascist war.'

They continued to affirm that the participation of the Soviet Union on the side of either the Axis or Allies would not change the character of the war as far as its imperialist allies are concerned, and that the duty of all revolutionaries was to defend the Soviet Union by every method of the class struggle and by the social revolution, notwithstanding their opposition to the bureaucracy, which must be overthrown by a political revolution.

We must also admit that the unification and the emergence of the EOKDE was a result of the necessity of having to resist the dictatorship, as well as the need for unity in the drive to build the Fourth International. The unification conference took place under conditions of extreme state terror.

In Greece, the Archeio-Marxist origins EOKDE had had a positive influence in that, ever since 1930, under the leadership of the International Left Opposition, they had sought unification on a Trotskyist basis. They were obliged to overcome the resistance to this unity of Pouliopoulos, who had aligned himself with the Landau-Nín tendency in the POUM. Pouliopoulos was by now a firm supporter of unity. In vain had Giotopoulos met with him in order to drive a wedge between the two tendencies. It must be added at this point that Giannakos' support for unity was very helpful throughout the whole period of discussions between the two tendencies.

Despite the dictatorship's repression, the first issue of *The Proletarian* was published in February 1937. About 80 per cent of it was written by Pouliopoulos, who was hiding all the while in the house of comrade Menelaos Megariotis' father. Those in the Acronauplia concentration camp, where most of the rank and file of the *New Course* and the Spartacists (Pouliopoulos' group) were imprisoned, were overjoyed when we heard of its publication, but we were unable to obtain copies.

The Proletarian was the only oppositional publication of a Trotskyist nature that was able to circulate during the first two years of the Metaxas dictatorship. It was duplicated and circulated by hand. The responsibility for publication rested with comrade Megariotis, one of the newer comrades, and the equipment was secretly guarded in a separate house. Demosthenes Vourzoukis, although an intellectual, was not among its usual contributors, as he was constantly on the move during the dictatorship in order to evade capture by the police. Neither were comrades Costas Anastasiadis and Vryhoropoulos, even though they also had the ability to write.

The Proletarian was published continuously until 23 June 1938, with 21 issues appearing. It only stopped when the entire Central Committee was arrested. The EOKDE continued for almost another year, supported by a handful of members who were still at liberty, most notably comrades Megariotis and Kondilidis. Here is a list of articles published in the paper:

February 1937: 'International developments and the political situation in Greece'; a resolution of the founding conference

March 1937: 'Revolution and counter-revolution in Spain'; 'A programme for immediate action by the organisation: To topple the dictatorship, for a new Communist Party, to organise a guerrilla movement'.

Issues 5, 6 and 7 are missing.

June 1937: 'The death agony of the Soviet bureaucracy'
Issue 9 is missing.

30 July 1937: 'Down with the hated Metaxas dictatorship'
26 August 1936: 'The Metaxas dictatorship masquerade'; 'Spain: July 1936-July 1937'

20 September 1937: 'The international campaign for the counter-trial and defence of Leon Trotsky'

28 October 1937: 'On the threshold of a new imperialist war'; 'The war and the tasks of Communists'

25 November 1937: 'The current situation and its significance for the dictatorship'

25 December 1937: 'And now, dangerous traitors'
5 March 1938: 'To topple the dictatorship'; 'To organise
the workers' United Front'; 'The Bukharin, Rakovsky and
Rykov trial'
20 April 1938: A leaflet.
25 May 1938: 'The king is having a good time -- for how
long?'; 'And the Black Knight'; 'Luxemburg's nightmare';
'The First of May'
28 June 1938: 'Down with the imperialist organisers of the
war'; 'Down with the dictatorship'.

The organisation continued its activities throughout the
period of illegality. The core groups carried out illegal
work in a Bolshevik spirit. The sections in Athens, the
Piraeus and Thessalonica worked in the usual manner. *The
Proletarian* was published regularly, and was passed on
from hand to hand, as where the duplicated declarations.
The workers did not hesitate for a moment to provide the
prisoners and exiles with material and food parcels. Illegal
articles were also sent frequently in double-bottomed
travelling bags. Documents were hidden in the soles of
shoes and ingenious hiding places in clothes.

The activities were easier in the suburbs and the factories.
The recruitment of those drawn towards us was checked
momentarily during this period, but it did not stop
altogether. The trade unions were viciously attacked. All
the left wing unions were dissolved. Some of them were
placed under appointed administrators, and became mere
paper organisations, only able to show banners on
demonstrations. The first blow was aimed at the bakers'
union, a stronghold in the trade union movement. The
Metaxas government and its Security Police had not

forgotten their humiliation in the great strike of April 1936, which was led by M Soulas (OKDE) and A Sakkos (*New Course*), and in which the workers were victorious. Some comrades, working in clandestine, held positions in Athens, especially in the employment organisations. Either as parties or individuals, we were all united in the fight against the right wing unions. Much the same occurred in Thessalonica. Later on, when the apparatus of the dictatorship and their quislings had been badly shaken, there were the strikes of the mill workers of the Piraeus under the leadership of comrade Smirlis, and in the German ships, led by Kleanthis.

In the Piraeus comrade Haritonidis led the construction workers' organisation and the workers' centre in Kokkinia, which he had established during 1928, despite the fact that he was taken every day to the Security Headquarters to be intimidated and forced to make a declaration. The same things happened to unskilled workers like V Nikolinakos, and to building workers like K Raptis.

The students' circle led by Demosthenes Vourzoukis were engaged in a similar struggle. In the circle were, amongst others, Andreas Papandreou, Kornelios Kastoriades, T Kirkos, Christos Karabelas and E Hierotheos.

Papandreou (future President of Greece in 1980's) had been influenced by Trotskyism since 1933. This was the time when Trotsky developed his analysis of Hitler's Fascism and his critique of Stalinism, and his books could be found in the library of Papandreou's father. Papandreou published two articles in a magazine called *New Beginning*, the same title as a pamphlet by Pouliopoulos, who had been the Secretary of the KKE, and who had resigned from the party in 1927. Papandreou was involved in the duplication of *The Proletarian* during the dictatorship, and his room was used as headquarters until his arrest with 12 other comrades, who were forced to sign a declaration of repentance. Kastoriades, (subsequently to become a famous French intellectual) who was good for nothing, signed an agreement as soon as he was arrested, and became anti-Soviet and later overtly anti-Communist as well.

Two further student circles were comprised of C Prikades, Nikolopoulos, the Oikonomou brothers, a student girl whose name I do not know, S Christopoulos, G Christopoulos, A Charalampopoulos, T Vourzoukis, T Lampropoulos and the famed Stratos Spanias, who was later murdered by the Stalinists. They were all arrested during a gathering which was held to raise money for prisoners.

In April 1937, during an official visit of Zan Ne, the French Minister of Education, the EOKDE encouraged the students not to welcome a minister of imperialist France, as the Stalinists did, but to show their disapproval of the Popular Front, and to take the opportunity to oppose the hated dictatorship. It was the centenary of the founding of the university, and Zan Ne placed a garland on the grave of the unknown soldier. The manifesto was circulated along with that of the Stalinists on that day, and posters supporting the dictatorship were torn down by the students. Further demonstrations against the dictatorship also occurred afterwards at Parnassos. K Kotzias, the dictatorship's minister, was booed at the stadium. These demonstrations ended with wild violence and mass arrests.

2. Arrest and Interrogation Oral Account - L. Karliaftis

I was one of the first to be caught. I fell into the hands of Kompoholi, a police captain who later became the commander of the Security Police. He was a dyed in the wool anti-Communist and a passionate persecutor of the working class and revolutionary movement. He was the right hand man of Maniadakis, the Minister of Public Security.

He recognised me, and then arrested me. I'd had trouble with him before. I had the honour to attract his anti-Communist hatred whilst he was a commander of the Security Police at Drama in 1929-30, six years previously. He had not forgotten me, and neither had I forgotten him!

I had been sent by the Archeio-Marxist organisation to head the Political Committee of East Macedonia and West Thrace. I was picked up as a foreigner at Kavala in a search conducted by Alexakis, who had the reputation of being one of the worst torturers and persecutors of Communists. His police and courts, which regularly sentenced people to from five to 10 years in jail, had gained control over the hitherto powerful tobacco workers' union, and he placed his committee men in every tobacconist shop.

I could not avoid arrest. I was tortured for two nights and a day by various modern methods. Despite sleepless exhaustion and intensive questioning, they got no information, neither a name nor a village! 'Where and with whom do you live?', they demanded. I told them, 'In a shed in the castle.' They searched it only to find it empty. I was then beaten mercilessly. How could I say that I lived with comrades? The only thing I didn't keep secret was my commitment to Communism. They searched for a false identity -- nothing! They asked Drama for more information -- absolutely nothing! But Kompoholis was the commander there, and he was another monster like Alexakis.

Kompoholis rushed to see me, to take over my interrogation. What a great honour for me! Finally Alexakis sent me to court. A move from hell to paradise! I was sentenced for one month -- for vagrancy! I enjoyed that. The lawyer, sent from the Stalinist-controlled Workers' Aid, 'defended' me like a bourgeois anti-Communist, treating me as he treated Stalinist defendants. He begged the court to be indulgent because I was 'foolish'. I stood up and repudiated this lawyer: 'I am neither foolish nor a tramp. I am a Communist and you can punish me for that!' The judges burst out laughing, much to the lawyer's embarrassment.

I continued to circulate our propaganda once I was released. I was captured at Xanthi in Alexandroupolis, beaten up and thrown out. They were satisfied with expelling me and removing me from their affairs.

I was arrested again at Drama, and brought before the court. Despite a lack of evidence, Kompoholis proposed a three-month sentence and then exile. The accusations concerning 'an independent Macedonia and Thrace' did not apply to us Archeiomarxists, as we considered that this had nothing to do with the slogan of the self-determination of the oppressed minorities.

When my sentence had finished, the commander of the jail handed me over to the Security Police for my exile. The Security Police headquarters, the court and the jail were in one compound, which at that time was full of people. The office of the commander of the jail was upstairs, and he was the first to go through the door. I suddenly had a bright idea. I turned around, rushed downstairs and mixed in with the crowd in the yard. I went straight out and walked to Kavala, an eight-hour walk. That's how I escaped from Kompoholis' clutches. But this encounter with Kompoholis resulted in my arrest during the Metaxas dictatorship, and a seven-year sentence in the concentration camps of Acronauplia and Pylos.

How Pouliopoulos, Giannakos, G Xipolitos and Giannis Makris, the heroes who fell under the Fascists' bullets at Nezero, were caught is a whole story in itself. This was the time when everyone was being caught. The arrests far exceeded the number of 50,000 militants reckoned in official statistics as having made declarations of repentance, apart from those, around 580, who remained a tower of strength in Acronauplia, facing torture and death, and another 1000 who were exiled on the islands. In Greece nobody could escape Maniadakis' numerous policemen, and all those who took fright made declarations of repentance, deserted and gave up the fight.
There was little working class resistance to the establishment of the dictatorship. The revolutionary movement, after the betrayal and defeat of the events of 1936 in Thessalonica, was in a disorganised retreat,

compounded by the effects of Hitler's rise to power in 1933, which spread confusion over the working class internationally, especially in the Communist movement. The 4 August coup was not, of course, Fascism, as the Stalinists stated with their theory of 'Fascism everywhere' which characterised all governments as such, and as did the defeatists such as Agis Stinas, who talked of 'red Fascism' in the Soviet Union.[1] It was a Bonapartist dictatorship, which is not to say that its methods were any different.

As I mentioned, I was one of the first to be captured by the dictatorship. Kompoholis had discovered where I was working. He had already met me in Kavala in 1930 in the prisons of the dreaded Alexakis. After the trials, the sentences, the discharges and the new arrests, this time in Drama, he came to provide the necessary information on my revolutionary credentials. Kompoholis and Alexakis had acted brutally in 1927, and since then had become the worst persecutors of the revolutionaries in Greece.

Kompoholis had sent a beast called Ioannides, who dragged me to the general Security Police. I conducted myself as befitting a leader of the Trotskyists of the *New Course*, as a Bolshevik. We were tortured, but not forced to drink castor oil. This was administered only by the special Security Police. We were exiled to St. Stratis. After the hell of the Security Prison, this exile was paradise. This was the second time I had been banished to St Stratis since 1935, when Kondilis had sent between 40 and 50 party leaders in one ship -- among them Varnalis and Glinos. He exiled us so that he could bring back the king without resistance -- which he then did.

Whilst the arrests continued and the dictatorship succeeded in disorganising all working class organisations, the Trotskyists managed to organise their unification conference. This was no mean achievement. We were the only party to hold a national conference under these unprecedented conditions.

The blows of Maniadakis soon fell heavily upon the EOKDE. Under intense surveillance, we began to tire. How could we avoid this? Day and night we attended meetings, distributed propaganda and engaged in all kinds of action. The Executive of the Bakers' Union instructed us to see their members, and at Tsakos, for example, we were betrayed by reactionaries, as in Christos Soulas' case. There was the vital necessity to bring our new members into activities, and to keep in touch with each other.

Giannakos was captured in Thebes, where he had gone to escape the repression in Athens. He was hiding in a house of some relatives, and was betrayed by one of them. Fortunately, he was able to save his books and papers. He refused to bend under torture, and was sent to Acronauplia. We cannot recall how Xipolitos and Makris were caught, theirs was just one in that mass of stories of life and death that circulated in Acronauplia. Raptis was caught immediately after the conference, as was Vitsoris, who had, together with Stinas, been in a minority in supporting incorrect political tactics and had left the *New Course*. Raptis and Vitsoris were freed, but Vitsoris had been ill-treated.

Tamtakos was caught whilst he was working at Sotiria in September 1937. He was detained for three months in a Security Prison, and then exiled to Giaros, where there was a whole group consisting of Tournopoulos, Pontikis, Diplas, Staphilatos, Giannakopoulos, Tasakis, Smilis and Lambropoulos.

Anastasiadis was captured at the end of September whilst he was on his way to a Central Committee meeting, and was sent to Acronauplia, where he remained for six months. L Vourzoukis was caught along with 10 other comrades, among them Nikos Aravantinos and Katina Megarioti. Thus with the arrest of Pouliopoulos that followed, the Central Committee of the EOKDE ceased to exist, as its members were sent to the concentration camps and into exile, and other comrades took on the responsibility for the continued existence and activities of the illegal organisation.

Pouliopoulos was captured at the beginning of 1938. He had been widely sought. The Security Police had set a prize of 20 000 drachmas for his arrest. Previously condemned to death during the war in Asia Minor, narrowly escaping a death sentence at a military tribunal of the 'democracy' when he was a Secretary of the KKE in 1925, a supporter of Bukharin in the staff of the Comintern only to be crushed in 1927, now he was the leader of the EOKDE with a big price on his head. This was only published in the *Police News* so that they would get the 20 000 drachmas, no mean amount. Ironically, this only appeared 10 days after he was caught.

To begin with, Pouliopoulos was hiding in the house of Megariotis, and had adopted the name of 'Petros'. This was in June 1937. Old Megariotis looked after him as if he was his own son, and he even held a birthday party for him on the Day of St Peter and Paul. He stayed there for a long time, but eventually his hideaway was discovered. The house was raided, but he escaped. Known to be wanted, Pouliopoulos was welcomed into the house of an intellectual, Karagiannis, an old follower, to whom I always gave copies of *Bolshevik* and the *New Course*. A good-humoured man, he was not in the party and so was not known to the Security Police. Pouliopoulos stayed at his house for a month, but then left. The sensitive Pandelis did not wish to task Karagiannis' pregnant wife any further. He thanked them warmly, and left. He went to comrade M, but he was also wanted, and he pointed Pouliopoulos to Sidiropoulos' house in Marousi. He was a tobacco worker with years of activity in the workers' movement, a supporter of Pouliopoulos. There were other tobacco workers in the area whom I knew from my Archeiomarxist activities in the Piraeus from 1927 to 1929, but only the splendid Kotsias knew of Pouliopoulos' hideaway. Pouliopoulos settled in that house, but was obliged to go out on party business.

In the meantime Lilis arrived at the house, breathless and under pursuit. Pouliopoulos considered him too excited, and that his condition would betray us. With nowhere else to run, he was allowed to stay. Kondilidis arrived a few days later. They could not stay at Sidiropoulos' house any longer. Kondilidis left, but Lilis and Pouliopoulos remained. Pouliopoulos used the name 'Pericles'. They accepted Sidiropoulos' proposal to move to one his comrades, the vegetable seller Sarifoglou. Megariotis arrived at this new hideaway. He had just had an operation in hospital when the Security Police entered his house looking for Pouliopoulos. They found him in the hospital, but they did not take him to the Security, and he immediately escaped to Thessalonica. He hid in the house of D Papadopoulos, an old trade union leader and follower of Pouliopoulos.

Before long the newspapers reported the arrest of some of the EOKDE Central Committee, with Demosthenes Vourzoukis as one of the first detained. Megariotis wasted no time, duty called in Athens. He discovered Pouliopoulos' telephone number from Stavros and called him up. They arranged to meet. Stavros was an old Archeiomarxist, and now a supporter of the *New Course*, enjoying the absolute confidence of Pouliopoulos. Stavros was also sought after and on the run. And so now there were Pouliopoulos, Megariotis and Lilis hiding in Sarifoglou's house.

However, Sidiropoulos had turned traitor. The hideaway was now a trap. The net around Pouliopoulos was tightening. The police were keen to catch him, not merely for 'patriotic' reasons, but also for the money. One day in early August a black car parked outside the house, and in it a gang of policemen. They knocked on the door and asked for Pericles. Pouliopoulos came out calmly. 'Which Pericles do you want? I am Pericles -- Pouliopoulos', he told them in the proud style of Roumeli. Thus was Pouliopoulos caught, and Lilis along with him. Megariotis had gone to Koptis, saw the black car on his return, and avoided arrest.

At the Security Police Headquarters Pouliopoulos asked the policemen who had arrested him whether they'd received the reward. 'It is complicated', they said. Who had betrayed him?

Karagiannis, Megariotis and M visited him separately at the Headquarters. He told them that the traitors were Sidiropoulos and Sarifoglou. He gave Megariotis a note with the name of the traitors to be given to the organisation. M, an old assistant of mine in the Piraeus, was above suspicion, as was, as far as I was concerned, Kondilidis. Vourzoukis thought that Lilis' telephone calls to the organisation from the Palataki tavern in the Piraeus could have led to the arrests, but I did not agree.

Megariotis and Kondilidis were two young men with an unshakable confidence in Trotskyism. Upon them fell the entire burden of the running of the leadership of the EOKDE after Pouliopoulos' arrest. They kept the organisation functioning and produced *The Proletarian*, the illegal paper of the Fourth International in Greece. The bitter campaign of the Security Police against the Trotskyists was intensified when a strike occurred at the Papastratos cigarette factory, which was organised and led by C. Antoniou, who was a former Archeio-Marxist and now a Trotskyist. This was too much for the Metaxas regime to tolerate. Antoniou was caught and tortured. Blows to the head left him deaf, and he was sent into prison and exile.

The Security Police wanted to report a complete success in every case. The Megariotis team, Kondilis and the

EOKDE university students, were caught. Originally the creation of the redoubtable Vourzoukis, this group was loved by all. Megariotis rebuilt the group, among whom was Andreas Papandreou. There was a duplicator in his room on which *The Proletarian* was produced, and Papandreou cut the stencils. Only Kondilidis knew of his room, and only Papandreou knew where he was working. Megariotis was caught at his work. Who betrayed him? A Security Police announcement read:

'After an extensive search, the Special Security Police arrested the following students who had formed an organisation of Fourth Internationalists, followers of the exiled Trotsky, led by the Communist Menelaos Megariotis, a chemistry student, who appears to be the Secretary of the Central Committee of the organisation. From the house of Andreas Papandreou was taken a typewriter and a duplicator, with which the illegal Communist paper *The Proletarian* was printed, along with various Communist papers and leaflets. Those arrested confessed their activities and, with the exception of Megariotis, submitted declarations of regret and a renunciation of their Communist views:

1. Andreas Papandreou
2. Cornelius Castoriadis
3. Kirkos Kirkou
4. Eleutherios -----
5. Christos Karabelas
6. Helias Kolovos
7. Ioannis Kontogiannis
8. Stefanos Gastratos -- all law students
9. Christos Valias -- a sixth-form student in the High School
10. Nikos Kondilis -- a student and electrician

11.Menelaos Megariotis -- a law student
Plus two or three others.'" (Athens, Greece August 1999)

3. **Acronauplia Concentration Camp - Greece**

Acronauplia was not, of course, as bad as Auschwitz or Dachau, but it was modelled upon the Fascist concentration camps. It was a Venetian castle, a medieval fort. An extension adjacent to it was first used as a barracks, and then as a conference centre. A prison for those serving hard labour sentences was built on a hill opposite the main prison, and being sent there was a virtual death sentence. Kolokotronis, the leader of the Greek revolution of 1821, had been imprisoned there. Acronauplia was first given the title of a prison for Communists, but it was not a prison. The prisoners were not there by order of a court, but by virtue of the decisions of Public Security Committees, or on the order of the Minister of Public Security, Maniadakis. There were many exiles among the detainees.

Eventually it was decided that the most apt term for the prison was that of a concentration camp, as in the Fascist countries. The authorities in Acronauplia attempted to enforce strict military discipline. Prisoners were isolated from the outside world. Correspondence, except two letters per month to one's family, was forbidden. Only family visitors were permitted, and they were persuaded and sometimes even threatened to try and make us sign declarations renouncing our principles and beliefs.

Oral Account - L. Karliaftis Life in the Concentration Camp Akronafplia

"After great efforts on our part, we were permitted to have a very few books, but no newspapers at first. Much later we were allowed to read a newspaper, but that contained nothing but Fascist poison. We had very little water at first, the time permitted for a walk in the prison yard was barely enough for us to stretch our legs, and we went hungry very often. A strict military discipline was imposed, we could not rise before reveille had sounded, and revolutionary songs were strictly forbidden.

At the beginning an internal guard was maintained. Every morning we were counted and reported on, with the prisoners standing to attention right through the proceedings. Bed-time and lights out regulations had to be obeyed without question. We protested and fought tooth and nail to break this unpopular Fascist barracks regime.

We acted very carefully to secure what freedom we could within those walls. The situation became critical. In September 1937 the prison guards attacked the prisoners, after having encouraged them to break the prison rules -- in other words, a provocation.

One night 'Göring' entered cell 2 and ordered us to stop what we were doing and go to bed, as lights out had been signalled. Nobody moved. He left and we heard a pistol shot. That was the signal for the guards to shoot. A hail of bullets hit the cells. They were shooting to kill. We were not frightened. On the contrary, we shouted back, 'Shame on you, murderers!' We crept under our beds, shielding ourselves with mattresses or stood in the corners or behind bullet-proof walls. This continued until Vrettos, the Prison Director, returned from Nauplia and ordered a cease fire.

This murderous assault cost the school teacher P Stavridis his life. His head was shattered as if it was a vase, and his brains spilled out onto the floor. The prison authorities said he was shot dead whilst trying to escape...

Raptis Pablo (leader of Fourth International after Trotsky's death) was exiled to Folegandros. He had not at that point signed any declaration of repentance. He did not take part in any of our meetings there. He was neither warm nor fraternal towards us. Was it his temperament? Was he pretending to be somebody else? Or did he have psychological problems? However, he did not give us the impression of being somebody likely to sign a declaration of repentance. Suddenly he left and was taken to the Ministry. After a while we heard that Maniadakis had freed him on condition that he went abroad. We were certain that he signed a declaration of repentance. It was well known that nobody had ever been released without signing one.

Meanwhile Vitsoris had been arrested, but through the mediation of the great actress Kotopouli, he had been freed to go abroad by Maniadakis, just as in the previous case of a highly esteemed member of the Glinos group, Likogiannis. The group's leadership had said nothing, but we knew that Maniadakis would not free anyone without obtaining a declaration of repentance.

We discussed the cases of Raptis and Vitsoris, but could not form a uniform opinion. The majority approved of the behaviour of Raptis, but not that of Vitsoris. Only Xipolitos, Tournopoulos and I condemned Raptis. These were times when those who signed a declaration were rejecting all their beliefs and convictions, and would lose the respect held towards those who remained in prison, facing death with courage.

Theodorou, the former Secretary of the OKNE (the KKE's youth group), who belonged to the Sklavos group, approached the prison authorities and asked for the records of the Raptis case. There he read:
'Maniadakis asked Raptis "Your parents have assured me that you were involved in the movement because you were young and immature, and that if I let you go abroad, you will never become involved again. What do you say?" He did not answer.' And as is very well known, he who remains silent, consents.

Raptis was not an ordinary member. He was a co-leader of the Pouliopoulos group, and a member of its Central Committee. Was it correct for the leaders to get a passport from Maniadakis and go abroad? And what about the ordinary members? Should they sign repentance declarations in order to leave? If the leaders deserted, should not the entire working class leave for abroad? If not, who would lead the working class to break its bonds? In this case Pouliopoulos showed all his greatness. To begin with, he had not heard of the affair. But prior to his capture he had met Raptis, who was by then freed. We never learned what Raptis told him or held back. Anyway Pouliopoulos brought the case before a Central Committee meeting, and Raptis' behaviour was condemned by Vourzoukis, Tamtakos and Anastasiadis. When Pouliopoulos was arrested, he was first taken to the Averof jail, and then to the jail on Aegina. From there he managed to send a letter to us at Acronauplia saying that 'Raptis is advising me to go abroad in the same way as he did. What is the opinion of the Acronauplia group?' We decided unanimously -- 'No'. Pouliopoulos had signed a contract of honour with the movement. He was not going to kneel before the ridiculous dictator. He had already started a struggle against the declarations of repentance, saying 'they can only take me abroad in chains, and even then I will find a way to return'. Our comrades abroad were not aware of how we were fighting against the declarations of repentance.

Raptis and Vitsoris were accepted abroad as representatives. But of whom, the Workers Front or *The Proletarian*? Nobody had nominated them as their representatives. Their behaviour abroad was irritating. Even during the dictatorship of Papadopoulos (1967) those abroad showed the same rotten liberal attitude, and today we know how much this costs. We have been heavily criticised over the matter of declarations of repentance. We know better than anyone else what we have lost, as the leadership of the international Trotskyist movement [in Greece] was wiped out. But we refused to reverse our decision. We believe that they had the same feelings on this as us. They are not dead, they live because their ideas live on"

3. The Founding Conference of the Fourth International

On 3 September 1938 the Trotskyist organisations assembled at a conference in France, and the Fourth International, the World Party of Socialist Revolution, together with the Youth International, was founded. Thirty representatives participated at the conference, from 11 countries: France, Britain, the Soviet Union, Germany, Belgium, Poland, the USA, Greece and various Latin American countries. It proved impossible to send representatives from Czechoslovakia, Spain, Austria, Indochina, China, French Morocco, South Africa, Canada, Australia, New Zealand, Denmark, Norway, Palestine, Lithuania, Romania and some of the other Latin American countries, as well as from the POUM and the PSOP of France, who had requested to attend as observers.

Never before had an international conference of such great significance taken place in a period of such immense difficulties provoked by the accumulation of the problems which foreshadowed the approaching world war.

The majority of the conference declared that the establishment of the Fourth International was an absolute necessity if there was to be any further progress of the revolutionary movement during this critical period. After a wide-ranging discussion the conference approved the programme of the Fourth International, *The Death Agony of Capitalism and the Tasks of the Fourth International*, written by Trotsky. The *Transitional Programme*, as it was popularly known, was based upon the first four congresses of the Third International. It is the *Communist Manifesto* of today, covering the entire epoch. The conference also voted to adopt the *Statutes* of the Fourth International, which were based upon democratic centralism.

Acutely aware of the approach of an imperialist war, the *Programme* declared:

'The bourgeoisie and its agents use the war question more than any other to deceive the people by means of abstractions, general formulae, lame phraseology, "neutrality", "collective defence", "arming for the defence of peace", "struggle against Fascism" and so on. All such formulae reduce themselves in the end to the fact that the war question, that is the fate of the people, is left in the hands of the imperialists, their governing staffs, their diplomacy, their generals, with all their intrigues and plots against the people.'[2]

It castigated the social patriots who were attempting to drag the exploited behind the war chariot in the name of 'democracy' and the Popular Front. It called on the working class to defend the Soviet Union, and called on workers to build a United Front against Fascism, to fight for the liberation of the colonial countries from imperialism, and to fight against the imperialist war and for the Socialist revolution.

The conference discussed the question of the unity of the Trotskyist movement in Greece, and decided that the unification of the EOKDE with the KDEE was necessary because the differences between the two organisations (the present situation in Greece and the question of the Archeiomarxists) did not justify the continuation of two separate organisations.

Without any authority Raptis dealt with the question of the entry of the POUM into the Fourth International, which had been proposed by the OKDE (Pouliopoulos and Raptis), in opposition to Trotsky, as well as presenting the question of Archeio-Marxism, which had been solved in 1930.

The conference declared that unification must take place on the basis of the *Transitional Programme*, and that the organisation would be known as the Revolutionary Socialist Organisation (Greek Section of the Fourth International). It added that a newspaper under a new name would be published, that a new temporary leadership would be formed on the basis of equality of representation, with the sanction of the International Secretariat, which would take decisions should disagreements arise between the two tendencies, that the members abroad would form a committee whose main duty would be to assist financially the Greek section and, in conjunction with the leadership inside Greece, prepare a conference of the new organisation, and that this committee would publish a magazine containing the documents of the two tendencies.

That this resolution, which was proposed by those two self-nominated 'representatives' Raptis and Vitsoris, was accepted by the conference was scandalous, because they had adopted the rôle of a political leadership, and yet, with the exception of the matter of unification, ignored the wishes of their comrades who were engaged in a life and death struggle under the dictatorship.

After the founding conference Raptis was kept in the sanatorium of the Yser, and had no -- absolutely no --

contact with any Trotskyist organisation, faithfully keeping the promise he had made to Maniadakis that he would not take part in any political activity. He was, therefore, unaware of and unable to participate in the conference which took place in January 1942 in Brussels, at which the European Secretariat was formed, and in which Marcel Hic, Yvan Craipeau and Zwan (France), Henry Opta and Abram Leon (Wajnsztock) (Belgium), and perhaps Martin Widelin (France) participated.

When Raptis realised that he could be accepted without any problems by the Greek section, he sent T Doris (Capnisi), who was given names and addresses, and who, as soon as he was arrested, betrayed to the Security Police comrades Prodromos Savas, Perkentes, T Giannopoulos, Prigouris and others. He also told them that Vitsoris had entrusted to Giannopoulos a case containing the organisation's archives, which were then seized by the spies.

5. Stalinism and the Second World War

The cohabitation group met once a month. The group's leadership did not want any political discussions at the meetings, least of all between EOKDE and the Stalinists. The camp was established whilst the civil war was raging in Spain, which, thanks to Stalin's sabotage, led to the defeat and destruction of the Spanish Republic and to Franco's victory. The consequences were grave in Greece, and in France where the way was opened for Pétain, and of course Hitler profited by this. What were the lessons of the Popular Front? Why did the Stalinists try to strangle any discussion on this subject?

Political Discussion in Akronafplia - L. Karliaftis Oral Account

"Everybody would talk during these discussions, but only for a minute or two. Political proposals were never adopted. The Stalinists tried to present both the domestic and international situations as favourable when in reality it was nothing of the sort. They believed that these lies would encourage their members and deter them from signing declarations of repentance. We told them that without a correct political orientation, and without any political guidance, Acronauplia, far from becoming a symbol of resistance, would merely represent the defeat of the working class. Unfortunately, that is exactly what happened.

There was no democracy in the cohabitation group, it was bureaucratic. Members had no democratic rights, they were turned into automatons. The Communist Party was the Central Committee, or to be more precise, the party was its leader Ioannidis. The group's leadership terrorised the members, and nobody dared to express his anxieties. Manousakas wrote:
'You needed great courage, as much as you would need in order to face your executioner, if you wished to defend the basic principle of Communism, that is democracy, within the party.'

Anyone who disagreed with the leadership was first of all expelled. Then he was branded a traitor, an agent of the Security Police, a spy, and was isolated from his comrades. You can imagine what it meant to be held in isolation, and unable to answer the charges and prove that you are innocent. They would also beat up anyone who disagreed with the leaders. There was no difference between the tortures of the Stalinists and of Maniadakis. Trivelas told me that the Stalinists had planned to kill Papagiannis in the Acronauplia bathroom, and only called it off when some of them objected.

The Molotov-Ribbentrop Pact of August 1939 shocked the Stalinists, although it wasn't so surprising for us. Trotsky had foreseen as early as 1933 that Stalin was seeking a way to come to an agreement with Hitler, so we were prepared for it. We later heard that in 1937 he had stated this to the Dewey Commission, and again in a speech to a group of US visitors to Mexico on 23 July 1939 -- precisely one month before the Pact was signed.[3] The Stalinists described the Pact as 'humanistic' and able to preserve peace, but this was shown to be false. No sooner had Molotov and Ribbentrop shaken hands than Hitler and Stalin invaded and partitioned Poland. The Pact was aggressive and expansionist. Hitler required the neutrality of the Soviet Union so that he could strike in the west. We already knew that Stalin had provided Mussolini with fuel when he invaded Ethiopia, and that he was only selling arms to the Spanish Republican government -- at double the normal price. Stalin was convinced that the Pact would prevent war with Germany. Despite warnings from his intelligence agents that Hitler was not intending to honour the Pact, he refused to prepare for war, and even started to praise the 'anti-imperialists' of Berlin and Rome.

As soon as the Pact was signed, the commander of Acronauplia camp deliberately announced the news to the prisoners. The Stalinists would not believe him, and asked to see the newspaper. He gave it to them and departed. Their confusion was indescribable. Most considered it to be a provocation, and some were getting ready to disavow Communism. We noticed their confusion and desperation, and started to discuss Trotsky's predictions with them. Manousakas wrote:

'At that time in Acronauplia, it was funny to see the anti-Fascists at loggerheads. Some were hoping for the victory of France and Britain. Others were wishing for the victory of the Fascists.'

Manousakas was among those loyal to the policy of anti-Fascism and democracy, and hoped for the victory of Britain and France. But Ioannides followed the Kremlin line, and the Greek Communists started supporting the 'hungry nations' and came out against the 'imperialists'. Neither presented a Socialist orientation towards the war.

The Trotskyists were the only organisation to hold a revolutionary policy towards the war. Lenin called for the transformation of the imperialist war into a civil war. We declared that both blocs were conducting a purely imperialist war, however they described it. We considered that war was a product of capitalism, and that Lenin, Liebknecht and Trotsky were correct in saying that the enemy was within our own country. Pouliopoulos had warned in June 1937 that there was no greater deceit than the insistence of the Stalinists and Social Democrats that the imperialists could fight an anti-Fascist war. He continued:

'And there is no greater deceit than the declaration that claims that the so-called Popular Front will save Europe from another war. The parties of the Popular Front, especially the Stalinists, are issuing increasingly chauvinist and nationalist propaganda under the banner of "defending democracy" in order to prepare ideologically the masses for the new slaughter. The imperialists -democratic and Fascist -- are preparing for war, and intend to drag the workers behind them. The biggest betrayal of the workers is being prepared today by the Stalinists and Social Democrats.'

Pouliopoulos wrote on 20 October 1937 that:
'We Communist Internationalists are the only people in Greece and all other countries who are fighting against capitalism and war. Let us consider the struggle against war as our paramount duty, and transform this war into a class struggle that will ensure the victory of Socialism and the establishment of lasting peace between all the peoples.'

We agreed with Lenin's policy of refusing to side with either imperialist bloc, and called for the defence of the Soviet workers' state. The Stalinists were unable to formulate a correct political orientation, and were therefore endangering the gains of the October Revolution. The Stalinist bureaucracy in the Soviet Union had to be overthrown, and Soviet democracy restored."

6. Neokastro Concentration Camp in Pylos

In the summer of 1939, on the orders of the Ministry of Security, 200 prisoners were taken from Acronauplia to an unknown destination.

L.Karliaftis recounts:"We said goodbye to our comrades with whom we had been incarcerated for nearly three years, full of anxiety and fear for what was awaiting us. You can imagine with what warmth we shook hands with our comrades whom we left behind.

We departed by night and reached Kalamata by dawn. The dictatorship had managed to turn the poor and the workers of Kalamata so much against Communism that they did not offer even a smile of sympathy when they saw us standing handcuffed in a long row. We were then taken on to Neokastro. The dispersal of prisoners from Acronauplia to Neokastro and other prisons on the islands was intended to divide them from those the authorities believed were their leaders, and so weaken the organisations.

Neokastro was a typical ruined Venetian castle, surrounded by very high walls topped with battlements. The cells were very small and damp. The strongest human would rot in these cells. This medieval grave was considered unfit for common criminals, but Metaxas' dictatorship had no qualms of using it for us. After all, he did not have the convenience of Dachau's crematorium.

There were four Trotskyists among the 200 prisoners: Giannis Makris: a fighter for 20 years. He originated in the general strike of 1923 in Pasalimano.

Christos Soulas: a young heroic baker who had participated in every struggle from 1926 until the day the dictatorship was established. He was executed in Kaisariani.

G Xipolitos: an heroic worker from the Piraeus who was executed along with Pantelis Pouliopoulos and N Giannakos in Nezero by the Italians.

Loukas Karliaftis: I was jailed alongside the leader of the Stalinists, Koligiannis, the successor to Zachariades. I had met him in 1935 on the island of Al-Stratis, where we shared the same room. We discussed privately there, as the Stalinists were not permitted to discuss with us.

We engaged in unarmed resistance in Neokastro. The men of Metaxas and Maniadakis tried to terrorise us by shooting at us from the top of the prison walls. We were unharmed because we were able to hide behind the walls of the cells.

A unique event took place in Neokastro camp. When the Second World War broke out, the prison commander called in the committees of the Stalinists and the Trotskyists, and asked them to express their positions on the war. Were we for or against it? Behind the question lay a deadly threat. Maniadakis wanted to destabilise the Communist Party, which was already divided. What would he do with those who would not submit? How would he treat the Trotskyists?

The Stalinist committee replied: 'Yes, we are on the government's side in the war against the Italian Fascists, and we ask to be sent to the front in order to fight them.' The prison commander then called on our committee. We had decided that Makris, Soulas and I should go. I answered in the name of the Trotskyists: 'No, we are against this war. This war is imperialist on both sides.

Greece is nothing more than a pawn on the Anglo-Saxon chessboard.'

He sent us away, rudely. We were sure that, at that moment, he was playing with our lives. But the men of Metaxas did not execute us. This criminal work was carried out by the Stalinists, much in the same way as Noske and Ebert had the Spartakist's murdered in Germany at the end of the First World War. The Stalinists murdered hundreds of Trotskyists because we fought to transform the imperialist war into a Socialist revolution.

Trotsky's *Manifesto of the Fourth International on the Imperialist War and the Proletarian World Revolution* of May 1940 declared:
'... we do not forget for a moment that this war is not our war. In contradistinction to the Second and Third Internationals, the Fourth International builds its policy not on the military fortunes of the capitalist states, but on the transformation of the imperialist war into a war of the workers against the capitalists, on the overthrow of the ruling classes of all countries, on the world Socialist revolution. The shifts in the battle lines at the front, the destruction of national capitals, the occupation of territories, the downfall of individual states, represent from this standpoint only tragic episodes on the road to the reconstruction of modern society.'[4]

Thirty-five years elapsed before we managed to get hold of this manifesto.

The social-patriotic sentiments which the Stalinists had spread around the world was not absent from the ranks of the Trotskyists, not least within James Cannon's Socialist Workers Party. Its *Statement on the US Entry into World War II* declared:

'Our programme against Hitlerism and for a workers' and farmers' government is today the programme of only a small minority. The great majority actively or passively supports the war programme of the Roosevelt administration. As a minority we must submit to that majority in action. We do not sabotage the war or obstruct the military forces in any way. The Trotskyists go with their generation into the armed forces. We abide by the decisions of the majority. But we retain our opinions and insist on our right to express them.'[5]

The anti-militarist struggle that was carried out in Neokastro and Acronauplia and on the islands was one of the brightest moments in the history of the revolutionary movement. The Greek Trotskyists honoured the flag of the Fourth International in a manner that few others did. Our bravery at Nezero and Kaisariani, and of those who died at the hands of the Stalinist social-traitors, together with those who survived, stood alongside Trotsky in a way nobody else did."

The highest number of casualties of trotskyists on an international scale after the USSR occurred in Greece where around 800 were executed during WWII by fascists and stalinists.

7. Stalinist Social-Patriotism in the Greek-Italian War

The Greek-Italian War was declared on 28 October 1940.
At that time the KKE's Secretary, Zachariades, was
imprisoned in Aegina. He showed his real character at this
critical moment. He had no principles. He instructed his
comrade Michailides to sign a declaration of repentance in
order to get out of the prison and rebuild the Communist
Party. Michailides left prison and became an agent of
Maniadakis. He set up a temporary party committee with
two or three others, and published the supposedly-illegal
Rizospastis. Behind all this stood Tyrimos and Manoleas,
former members of parliament who had become agents of
the Security Police. Now Zachariades knew all about this,
but he preferred to have a party led by police agents than
nothing at all. He produced a declaration on 31 October
1940 which read:
'The Greek people are fighting a war of national liberation,
led by the Metaxas government. We must all do our
utmost, without hesitation, to support it. The outcome will
be a new, free Greece, free from any foreign imperialist
dependence.'

Meanwhile, after Siantos had been arrested, an illegal
Central Committee had been established at the end of
1939. Its leader was Papagiannis and its members were
Ktistakis, Karvounis and Kenakis. They published an
illegal *Rizospastis*, of which very few copies appeared.
Zachariades' declaration, however, was widely broadcast,
unlike any other party material, because it was very useful
to the government. By now we had two Communist

Parties, each of which were accusing one another of being police agents.

There were 185 Stalinists in Neokastro. Half of them supported the temporary committee of Michailides and Zachariades, whilst the others remained loyal to the committee of Ktistakis and Papagiannis. They faced a real dilemma: was it an anti-Fascist war of national liberation or was it an imperialist war? If it was an anti-Fascist war, then how could they surrender to one dictator in order to fight another, Mussolini?

The Stalinists in Acronauplia prepared a memorandum for Maniadakis, asking him to release them for military service. All the Stalinists were asked to sign it, which they did. At the end of January 1941 General Ageletos was sent to Acronauplia by Metaxas to discuss with the group's leadership. After hearing them, the general assured them that he would ask for their release and despatch to the front. 'I wish Russia would help us', he added. But nobody was released, not even Zachariades, who after this changed his position, saying that the war was no longer defensive because the Greek army had crossed the border, and that it could no longer be called an anti-Fascist war.

Everybody in Neokastro was celebrating the victory of the Greek army, except the Trotskyists, who kept their minds on the revolutionary Socialist way out of the war. They were not pinning their hopes on the victory of Greek capitalism or of the imperialist western Allies, but only of the Soviet Union, the only workers' state. They believed that a genuine victory could only emerge from a revolutionary struggle against the war, which would bring lasting peace and real social liberation.

L. Karliaftis Account of Trotsky's Death...

"We were in Neokastro when we heard the news of Trotsky's death. We all gathered on 22 August 1940 in a room to read the newspaper. It was the most dramatic day of our lives. Trotsky was murdered by Ramon Mercader, alias Jacques Mornard or Frank Jacson. He had gained admission to Trotsky's house by posing as one of us, and had given him the deadly blow to the head. We were astonished and shocked. I do not know if our eyes were full of tears, but Bolsheviks have learned not to cry. We heard some people laughing, and we saw others smiling. Others had a look of triumph about them, like a wild beast that has just torn its prey to pieces. We felt that the eyes of all the Stalinists were upon us.

After reading the newspaper, we walked up and down the yard in silence. We had many thoughts in our minds. How was it possible? How did the murderer get in? How could the victor of October and the Civil War lose the battle? What effect would it have on our movement? At that moment we did not think that Trotsky's murder would mark the beginning of another great slaughter of the Trotskyists in Siberia, Greece, Indochina and China.

On 29 January 1941 we left our cells and saw the Greek flag flying above the administration offices. What could it mean? We were told that Metaxas was dead. That at least was one dictator less. The Metaxas dictatorship was over, but the covert royal dictatorship remained. This could only be overthrown by a workers' revolution."

8. Hitler's Occupation

The situation changed dramatically when the Germans invaded. Gone were the triumphal descriptions of successes in Albania. The front line in Albania collapsed, and the victors were vanquished. The army was demoralised, and hungry and bare-footed soldiers took the road of retreat. The government could not provide protection or help because it no longer existed. The country was in a state of chaos. The fear of death infected the entire population. Hitler had destroyed the pride and courage of those who had until lately been the victors. Even the bravest of them were confused and did not know how to face the enemy. The German tanks and Stukas terrified everybody.

At that time we were in Neokastro. About 200 Stalinists and Trotskyists were crammed into tomb-like cells. We were told to prepare ourselves -- but for what? And where were we to go? The Germans were approaching, and they would conquer everything. Then, as there were not now enough guards to keep them in, the authorities decided to close Neokastro camp. They were brought back to Acronauplia, even those condemned to death, travelling in two groups as there were not sufficient guards to keep them in one group.

L. Karliaftis recounts the story of Hitler's occupation and the effect in the concentration camp he was in:
"I swear that none of the 200 prisoners were afraid. We were all accustomed to the threats of the reactionaries, and

we had not been broken. We had faced the Italian bombs without fear. We were all very moved when we left Neokastro. We did not speak at all. We had until then considered it as our home, terrible as it was. We had spent bitter times in it, and yet there had been dramatic and beautiful times as well. We had survived the war there and witnessed its horrors. We had learnt there that the dictator Metaxas had at last died. We had fun when the Stalinists pleaded with the government to release them so that they could fight the Germans and defend their country. We had put our lives in great danger when we proclaimed ourselves against the war. And it was there where we heard the terrible news that Trotsky had been assassinated. That made Neokastro unforgettable, the worst news that we heard during those hard times.

Maniadakis had ordered the dispersal of Neokastro camp, and that all the prisoners at Neokastro and Acronauplia be handed over to the Germans. He then made his own escape. We were ordered to move. We Trotskyists, who were in the first group, were to go to Kalamata by bus, and then by train to Acronauplia. Our journey went smoothly, but the other group stayed until night in Kalamata as the trains could only move under the cover of darkness, due to the bombing. But Argos was bombed, and all the prisoners, guards and other people sought shelter in the fields. Antonatos wrote:
'On our way we removed our handcuffs. The gendarmes and their officer watched us, but they were so confused that they didn't know what to do. Once the raid was over we surrendered to the gendarmes, who handcuffed us again and took us to Acronauplia.'

Mamalakis, who was also in Neokastro, was asked by Manousakas: 'Why have you come to this hell?' He replied: 'We have come here to continue the struggle against you!' Koligiannis and Zisis Zisimatos, who were the leaders, had refused a request by their comrades to sanction an escape attempt. 'No', they said, 'we shall go to Acronauplia first, and then decide what to do.' They were like sheep to the slaughter. Ioannides approved this treason.

In the meantime, we were discussing how we could attempt to escape. Such thoughts were on everyone's minds. But the wise leaders recommended that we, the mere rank and file, should not discuss it, such things should be left to the leaders. But they did not raise the matter. 'Why didn't you escape?', asked Papadakis of his comrade Manousaka, 'Who told you not to escape?'

The gates were half open, there weren't many guards, just the commanding officer and 10 gendarmes, and the gendarmes were indifferent. They just wanted to go home. There was a threat that if anyone left he would be killed at once. But all the Stalinists knew that was an idle threat, they all knew that an escape would be dead easy. Yianigonas wrote: 'We could have escaped without facing any resistance, and we would have saved so many lives.'

We Trotskyists were more isolated than ever from the Stalinists, and we were unaware of their confusion. We did not know that some of them were of the opinion that they should escape. Manousakas refers to 10 Cretans who wanted to escape. Certain Stalinist leaders, Siganos, Soukatzidis, Chitilos, Karadonis and Mariakakis, to name some of them, also held this opinion. But Koligiannis instructed his men to stay put. And they did! What a shameful obedience to party discipline and the laws of the government.

The respect shown by Ioannides and Koligiannis for the law and the camp commander drove to the point of madness those Stalinists who wanted to escape. But, because of the Hitler-Stalin Pact, the Stalinist leaders were under the illusion that the Germans would not be hostile to them. They justified that wicked alliance in the same way that they had previously justified equally wicked alliances with imperialists against Hitler. They thought that the Germans would play fair with Stalin and, therefore, themselves, and at the worst would not execute them even if they did not let them free. They believed the 'poor countries' such as Germany and Italy to be in the right against the other imperialist countries of Western Europe. They even believed at that time that Hitler's nationalism was some kind of Socialism!

And so they waited for the Germans to come, explaining that 'if we got out of here, the British who are still in Nauplia would arrest us'. Manousakas wrote in his *Acronauplia: Tales and Reality*:
'There were others who took seriously the rumours which the committee of the party deliberately spread that the Germans were a highly civilised people and would treat us in a civilised manner. We were left to suspect that the agreement of Hitler with Stalin would become an alliance. I think the party leadership was responsible for this incorrect and immoral view. Unfortunately, we paid for that with the massacre of hundreds of prisoners, and we

also lost the possibility of gaining the control of the government.'

The frontier collapsed and the German tanks drove forward. The Stukas maintained an ever-increasing attack on Acronauplia. Many of the soldiers with their officers and the politicians were embarking at Anapli during the night to set sail for Crete or Cairo. A large number of British troops were killed as they embarked. A ship containing 400 tons of nitro-glycerine as well as soldiers was attacked by Stukas, and it exploded after the troops had escaped. The explosion rocked Acronauplia like an earthquake, and iron debris rained down on our building. Two troopships were sunk, and the beautiful harbour that we had enjoyed looking at became a sea of floating corpses. The Stukas kept up their attack, striking at a large beached ship until they realised that they could not sink it. We lived amongst all the horrors of war until the Germans finally took Nafplio.

We sheltered during the raids in a ditch which we had dug. By now there were over 560 prisoners, perhaps 600 in all. We and about a further 600 were all that remained of the Communists, both young and old, who had not submitted to dictator Metaxas. Amongst them were the tested militants who had fought for Communism for 20, 30 or more years, and who had been in prison or exile for many years. They had suffered persecution and torture. They had made many sacrifices for Communism, they had experienced the first awakening of the proletariat and its first struggles and revolts. And they were fearless.

Acronauplia had become a legend, a bastion of Communism, and a symbol for the struggles in the future. But the prisoners of Acronauplia, who had inspired people and who had suffered so much under the dictatorship, were betrayed by their unworthy leadership. The truth is that Stalinism destroyed them because its supporters submitted to a corrupt leadership.

The prison guards were in a complete state of panic during the bombing. They hid in their shelters, more interested in their families than in us. Nobody knew what would happen to us under the Fascists. During one raid, and while the Nazis passed through the Isthmus and took the Peloponnesus, we were in our shelter when we heard a voice in a sudden silence. It was Pouliopoulos. He spoke calmly and steadily:
'We must decide here and now how we are going to escape. The guards are in a terrible panic and so disorganised that we can surely escape. Otherwise they will deliver us up to the Nazis.'

His authority was impressive. So spoke the former Secretary of the Communist Party. His proposition went to the depths of our souls. Not a whisper could be heard. We were all waiting for the Stalinist leaders to speak.

I took the opportunity to speak. It was dark but they recognised my voice. I had always spoken as the representative of the Trotskyists. I had always lashed the Stalinists during the discussions, although they had only ever given me four minutes in which to speak. But they respected me. I was in my fifth year of imprisonment in the concentration camps of Acronauplia and Neokastro, and during those five years they had learned to respect me as a leading revolutionary. I said loudly:

'We must decide to escape without hesitation. That is our revolutionary duty. Great struggles lie ahead of us. Our success will be certain, and it will cost us no blood at all. Don't forget that the gendarmes just want to go home. We must be daring.'

There was complete silence for a while. The Stalinist leader Theo's not only refused to consider our proposal, but attacked us. 'Your proposition is a provocation. It is intended to put the collective in danger.' He told us that the commanding officer had given his word that he would not deliver us to the Germans, and that as soon as the British departed, he would set us free. The proposal to escape was a provocation! That was an ugly accusation, a slander against the efforts we had made for the safety of the lives of hundreds of class fighters, the finest members of the workers' movement.

If we had decided to escape, there is no doubt that we would have succeeded. The gates leading to the camp commander's office and the outside were almost always ajar as the trusties like Arabatzis and Archivasilis regularly went shopping with small or large groups. We could have quickly disarmed the guards, and if they had resisted, we could have seized the two machine-guns which stood in the corner of the office. There were 600 of us, and there were several guards who told us to escape because they wanted to come with us. Our escape would have been successful.

Had the followers of Theos and Ioannides not capitulated to them and not believed the words of that Greek officer, who was one of Maniadakis' narks, we all could have escaped without any blood being spilt at all. Some of them had been won over to our idea. Giannogonas wrote much later that they had planned an escape based on what we had said, but that Ioannides had cancelled it at the last moment. Moreover, Manousakas had said that there were some gendarmes from Crete in Nauplia who would help us to escape. But instead of sending Manousakas to Nauplia to arrange this with them, Ioannides sent Archivasilis, whom the gendarmes did not know and therefore would not trust.

In the meantime the Stalinists had posted their own guards over the gates in order to prevent both ourselves and their own members from escaping. Escaping was 'provocative' because this would put our 'freedom' in jeopardy and reverse our 'gains'. Our 'freedom' and 'gains' in the concentration camp!

Now was the opportunity for all of us to escape. But as soon as the old guards were paralysed we had new guards, and they were Stalinists, exactly like Zachariades. The Stalinist leaders Ioannides and Theos had thwarted our plan to escape. But how could this have happened? The reason is that they had fatal illusions in Stalin's allies, the Nazis, that they would treat us as if we were their allies as well. Their worship of Stalin created their illusions in Hitler. I remember trying to explain in vain to a Stalinist worker, who shared my cell, that Hitler would become a super-Wrangel against the Soviet Union, as Trotsky had foretold. The crimes of the Stalinists in Acronauplia had their roots in the general policy of the Kremlin."

9. The Assassination of Pouliopoulos - Main Leader of Greek Trotskyism

On 6 June the Italian Fascists executed on the hills of Kournovo 118 militants, and among them were the Trotskyists Pouliopoulos, Xipolitos, Giannakos and Makris, as well as the Trotskyist Archeiomarxist Lambropoulos.

L. Karliaftis Account of the Execution:

"We were all deeply shocked. We had felt the same blow when, in the camp at Neokastro, we heard of Trotsky's assassination. A cloud of death covered Kournos, and we cursed long and loudly.

By this time we were imprisoned in the camp at Larissa, which had been transformed into a fortress, with six lines of barbed wire, a watch tower every 15 or 20 yards and a light machine gun in each watch tower. There were more than 3000 inmates. When the Trikkala concentration camp was closed out of fear of local resistance, the prisoners were moved to Larissa. The camp was guarded by Italian soldiers.

The Stalinists who, under the leadership of Ioannides, had refused to escape from Acronauplia, were brought to Larissa. Their secretary was Koulambas. Among them were Siantos, Partsalides, Apostolou, Grigoratos,

Ikonomides and some others. They were in the central block, but not, of course, with the common prisoners.

In isolation in the lower part of the hut were our people, together with a dozen Stalinists who had been isolated by the others and had joined the Trotskyist and Archeio-Marxist collective.

Pouliopoulos had a great influence on the whole camp. He had contacts with all the politically aware prisoners, anti-Fascists, left wing activists, intellectuals and workers. Everyone liked and admired him for his revolutionary spirit, his philosophy and his talents. He inspired confidence in the workers' revolution and revolutionary future to come. He strengthened the morale of the weak and tired. His greatness impressed everybody. How many times did we hear them say: 'What a man that Pouliopoulos is!'

More than ever the Stalinists found themselves isolated from the other prisoners. They tried in vain to isolate our people. Their uncontrolled hatred and malice came to the surface whenever they were criticised by revolutionaries. Their hostility to all our people was a thousand times worse than at Acronauplia. The more Pouliopoulos attacked them for their social patriotism, their collaboration with the western imperialists, their submission to Greek capitalism and all their other betrayals, the more their hate for him grew. Their savagery knew no bounds.

When Thanos Georgiades, the son of G Georgiades, the old leader of the Socialist Party, arrived in the camp,

Siantos gave him his top bunk while he took the bottom one, but he said to him: 'Above all don't go near that Pouliopoulos.' Partsalides too said to him: 'Follow your father's heart but not his head.'

When Georgiades had gone to defend Pouliopoulos, who was facing the death penalty for treason at the trial of the autonomists, he had been a 'Social-Fascist' as far as the KKE was concerned. When Georgiades' daughter, sent by her father, visited Pouliopoulos in hospital, he said to her: '"Your father saved my life when he defended me at the court-martial during the dictatorship of Pangalos. Tell him that I thank him!" And now in the concentration camp, Thanos Georgiades, whom I knew as a convinced Socialist close to Trotskyism, is not allowed to go near Pouliopoulos.'

Nikos Simos, a long-standing Archeiomarxist and Trotskyist, had been arrested on 6 January 1943. He had been denounced as a Trotskyist to the Piatsa commando. He was questioned and tortured but they had no proof. They continued because he refused to sign a declaration denouncing Communism. They took him to prison at Calithea. There he met Thanos Georgiades. Three months later he was taken to the camp at Larissa. Nikos was known and loved by all. The Stalinists knew him very well. They feared him. The Trotskyists knew him under the name 'The Cook'. He was honoured for his fidelity to our ideas and his bravery.

The Stalinists refused to admit him into their area when the police had taken him there. Koulambas, the Secretary of the Stalinist group, said to him: 'You cannot join us until you state that you will not speak to Pouliopoulos.' Simos refused, and he was eventually taken from the common criminal section, where he had originally been put, to the Trotskyist and Archeiomarxist collective. Pouliopoulos welcomed Simos there. He knew him from the famous trial of Communists after the prison mutiny of Assos. Simos slept next to Pouliopoulos. There were 34 Stalinist and Trotskyist prisoners, among whom were Pouliopoulos, Giannakos, Xipolitos, Simos, L Chimaras, E Petsis, Belosimbassis and others.

The Assos prisoners had mutinied and refused to work in the fields. The prison commandant had accepted this at first, but later cut off all their communication with the outside world, letters, visits, etc, and had built a wall to isolate them from the criminal prisoners. He summoned and arrested the secretary of the collective. The prisoners rushed the commandant's offices. They were fired on. Bratsos was arrested and tied to a tree. In reply the Communists seized a policeman and demanded the release of Bratsos. Reinforcements were sent from all over Cephalonia, and they attacked. They fired on the prisoners, who fought back with their bare hands. Simos was wounded in the hand. The Stalinists Papavasiliou, Petros, Bavos and Armenis were also wounded. Eventually the rioters were dispersed, and the wounded taken to the hospital at Argostoli.

At the trial following the Assos affair, Pouliopoulos, the lawyer of the detained mutineers, together with the Stalinist barristers Porphyrogenis and Miliaresis, put forward a formidable defence. Pouliopoulos shocked the whole public and even the judges with a submission which lasted for two hours.

When the prison at Trikkala was closed, all the prisoners were taken to Larissa. Among them were G Makris, C Soulas, G Krokas, Spaneas, C Hadgichristos, E Petsis and Socrates, and all those who had not escaped from Evia with Pouliopoulos such as Giannakos and Xipolitos.

Our people were very effective in carrying out agitation and propaganda work among the 3000 prisoners. Every evening long talks and discussions took place, and Pouliopoulos impressed everyone with his knowledge. Every day the police brought between 200 and 300 prisoners back and forth to work on the aerodrome, Pouliopoulos and Giannakos as intellectuals were not so strong, but worked hard. They dug and piled up the earth next to me. As much as I was able, I helped them to rest. It was the same with Hadjichristos, Soulas, Makris, Petsis and even Krokas, as they were strong working men. They managed well despite all they had suffered in prison and exile. The guards kept us under constant surveillance, so nobody could avoid working by slacking.

During our work we argued softly with the Stalinists, unlike inside the camp where we could not speak. Their bosses were bothered if we even greeted each other. Every evening when they spoke with each other they came to blows. They wished to weaken those who rebelled against their reign of terror.

The Italians often amused themselves with songs and music at a nearby tavern, and brought prostitutes there. If there were no Germans with them they would have been helpless. Among the prisoners were five or six Englishmen. They escaped by bribing the Italians to get their German colleagues drunk.

A riot of all the prisoners, Stalinists and ourselves, took place. We beat up the Vlachs, who were the camp informers and who did a lot of harm to everyone. The guards called us to a general parade. They put us in line and the Italian commandant walked along it with a Vlach to identify which one of us had beaten him up. He pointed out a Piraeus cobbler and two others. They were violently beaten and taken away as if dead, the cobbler to the hospital. Afterwards they were put in solitary.

One night at half past one in the morning we heard screams and sobbing outside the camp, waking us all. Pouliopoulos managed to discover what was happening. Two trucks of Italians had brought in 200 children of between eight and 12 years old. Some had fainted, others were dumb with fear, and others wept and cried. In revenge for the killing of three of their soldiers by the resistance, the Italians had attacked the three neighbouring villages, and had killed everyone they found and then burnt the bodies. They had seized the children, terrified at the massacre of their parents, and had brought them to the camp by truck.

Pandelis was overcome when heard this, and exploded: 'The brutes! The murderers!' He then turned on the Stalinists: 'The filthy maquis!' It was a really bad method of struggle. The maquis killed three soldiers and the Fascists massacred and burnt three villages, and hundreds of children were orphaned. There was not a single act of fraternisation between the soldiers of the two sides against their officers, such as Leninist principles demanded. This was clearly as much a crime by the leadership of the social patriotic maquis as that of the Fascists.

The Trotskyists condemned the policy of unjustified sabotage and assassination of German and Italian soldiers to assist the war effort and the victory of the imperialist Allies, even when this was done on the pretext of helping the USSR, because this tactic led to a confrontation between the local workers and the German and Italian soldiers, deepened the gulf between them, destroyed internationalist perceptions, pushed the German and Italian soldiers towards the Fascists, and laid the basis for the destruction of the Greek, German, Italian and world revolutions. The tactic of sabotage is acceptable when it is included in a strategy of working class revolution by the masses, but sabotage in the service of the capitalist war has nothing to do with revolution.

The Stalinists did not worry about this sort of problem. But what about the 3000 prisoners who were in danger of being condemned to death if a train was sabotaged or another incident took place?

In June another event took place which aroused the anger of Pouliopoulos, and led to the catastrophe of Nezero. The local maquis learned that on the afternoon of 3 June 1943, a train loaded with Italian war material would be travelling by. They mined the line at St Stephen's cutting to cause a landslip and block the line.

On the train there were 1500 soldiers who did not know that the wagons were full of munitions. They were facing certain death, not just because of the saboteurs' charge, but because of the explosion which it would set off.

On 3 June at 5pm, the train entered the cutting. Shortly after a tremendous explosion occurred. It was hellfire. The wagons were blown to pieces, human bodies were broken into flesh and blood, and there were cries of pain for help. There were 600 dead and a great many wounded.

We were intensely depressed when we learnt of the sabotage. The Fascists had already compiled and publicised in the press a list of prisoners who would be executed if there was sabotage on the railway.

The news of the sabotage was a death sentence for the prisoners in the camp. The comrades on this list prepared for their execution, wrote their last letters to their dear ones and embraced their friends. Their last salute to life was without fear or tears.

Next day, 4 June, nothing happened, but the mood in the camp was sombre. The shadow of death hung over every head. On 5 June the police arrived with a dozen lorries. The atmosphere was tense. The condemned thought this was the end.

They called the morning parade very early. The commandant ordered the prisoners to stand in line outside their huts. There was a deathly silence and he started to read out the list. But the names were different. Not one of the names on the original list was called.

An article, 'A great and tragic anniversary' appeared in the local paper *Larissa* on 26 June 1979. It stated:
'The prisoners were ordered to their places outside their huts in the camp and there the commandant started to read out, not the names of those on the list, but other ones. What had taken place? How and who had changed the list? Was the change the result of some evil influence?'

Hopes rose. Perhaps they were not going to be executed. They collected their belongings. They shook the hands of their comrades, climbed into the lorries and left. For where?

They returned to the camp that evening, feeling relieved. What had happened? Read the explanation in *Larissa* on 25 June 1979...
"How were the names on the first list changed, the Trotskyist leaders entered and the KKE leaders omitted? The leaders of the EAM have forgotten this question in the same way as they forget the great massacre of Trotskyists on the eve of the revolution, when we found ourselves in the front line of the barricades with the rebellious masses against the murderous attack of Papandreou and Scobie, when the activists of ELAS took to us to the OPLA and Peoples' Militia firing squads."[6]

For a long time nothing was learned as to why the names on the execution list were changed. Then Felicia Pouliopoulos, the widow of Pantelis, brought the crime carried out against our comrades at Larissa concentration camp by the Stalinists out of the shadows.

Among the Stalinist leaders there was Zographos, a would-be intellectual cadre, a veteran 'Trot-basher' from Acronauplia. After the betrayal of Pouliopoulos he bribed the Italians responsible with party gold in order to include Pouliopoulos and any others of our comrades on the lists for future executions. It is quite possible that this horrible act was carried out by the interpreter who, according to Simos, was one of the most disgusting people he had ever encountered.

Felicia Pouliopoulos subsequently split from the Athanassiadis tendency and defected to the Stalinists with Dimitrakareas. What had she learnt, before or after she had joined the Stalinists? We heard this from a relative of Pouliopoulos. Felicia will not tell me any more details. She may not, of course, agree with what happened then, or perhaps she has been threatened with expulsion if she told us what happened.

But returning to the prisoners at Larissa, not all shared the optimism of their comrades even though a guard said to one of them as they climbed down from the lorries: 'You are in luck! Do you know where we were taking you?' 'No', replied Pouliopoulos who spoke Italian.

'To Kournovo -- for execution!' 'Why then, what has happened?'
'It seems that the execution has been cancelled.'

But it was not. The execution had only been delayed because of information that the maquis were intending to free them. From Athens came the order to execute them the next day. On the night of 5-6 June nobody was able to sleep. Simos tells us movingly:

'Lying by Pouliopoulos' side I felt the need to say a few comforting words to him, even though he did not seem upset. "Perhaps you are going to be transferred to another prison." "Stop it Nikos", interrupted Pantelis, "I have heard it with my own ears that they are going to execute me."'

Simos stopped and burst into tears. That is what the interviewer and the wife of Simos Vassiladiotis heard. When he stopped Nikos continued:

'Yes it was true. Pantelis knew it. He had heard two policemen discussing among themselves saying, "Ah, if this execution didn't go ahead, we would have a party with a roast lamb." Perhaps they were not anti-Fascist but simply human. Another time Pantelis said to me: "Bad luck Nikos, I won't be able to go on arguing about Archeiomarxism, as I hoped."'

We did not know how Archeio-Marxism had evolved of late as a consequence of events. Since Acronauplia they had had a new experience by collaborating of our tendency, the *New Course* in the EOKDE, while the tendency of Pouliopoulos had evolved in two different and opposite directions. This conversation shows that Pouliopoulos was concerned with the problems of our struggle right to the end.

At dawn on 6 June the klaxon sounded. They called out those on the list. It was the last 'Present' in their life, and the first in eternity.

The lorries returned, but there was a delay in the order to depart. They waited until midday. This was the worst sort of torture experienced by all those who had been held in the police jails. The agony was felt not just by the 150, but by all 3000 prisoners.

At last the time came. The order to go was finally given. In the dormitories the heroes of Nezero embraced all their friends one after the other: 'My love to the children', 'Have a good Liberation.'

The scenes of the departure were dramatic. They did not have the cheerful character of normal transfers between prisons and exile. It was extraordinarily sad. But there was one peculiar thing. The expressions of all showed something of revolutionary purity and greatness. Stalinists and Trotskyists marched as one, proudly and without fear.

'When those about to die came to Kournovo', wrote Olympios in *Larissa*, 'they were lined up by the side of a little hill facing the machine guns. Before the execution started Pouliopoulos shouted out in Italian: "You have learnt to scorn death while we scorn life!"'

An Italian anti-Fascist from the Pinerolo Cavalry Brigade who after the fall of Italy went over to ELAS with his men and 8000 horses, described the execution to the leading ELAS people at the their officers' school:
'Pouliopoulos had a hero's attitude. He said in Italian: "In killing us you kill yourselves -- you are fighting against the idea of the Socialist revolution."'

The scene of the execution was not a drama but a Golgotha, different from the hundreds of executions of the National Resistance.

Pouliopoulos gave a message to the Italian soldiers, a message of brotherhood to all the soldiers of the earth, whether white, black or yellow, above frontiers and parties. A message of revolution against the hell of capitalist war. His appeal was the correct appeal of a war against war. He wanted to bring down the high and mighty, to raise the oppressed peoples against imperialism, and to raise Siberia against the Kremlin.

It was a clarion call in the spirit of the Russian October -- peace to the peoples, world revolution, down with all the despots of the globe -- and all in a few firm words before the order to fire.

At Nezero Pouliopoulos wrote an eternal message with his blood, like that of the Chicago martyrs or the Communards of Paris, shot by the 'democracy' of Thiers.

He has taken his place at the tribune of the world revolution. His appeal was a call to struggle. He saw the soldiers not as assassins but as his brothers. The real executioners and assassins were in the general staffs, and not just in those of Hitler but in those of Churchill and Roosevelt.

I remember when the Germans came to Acronauplia and calmly looked at us behind the bars, without any dislike, Pouliopoulos said: 'What pleasant blond faces.' They were all young. Hitler had called up deskrows of schoolkids to send to the front.

It took at least five minutes to execute them all. Pandelis did not go down until the last second. He had heard that there were Italians who would celebrate with a roast lamb if the execution did not take place, and he aimed his words at their hearts and consciences. He was hopeful, and in no unrealistic way, for from June to September, when Mussolini was overthrown, the Italians fraternised, and anti-Fascism conquered the whole of Italy.

'Brothers...', Pandelis spoke slowly. The emotion of the speaker was palpable. He spoke to his friends on the other side. Our Socialism has taught us to extend our hand to our comrades against all class enemies.

We can imagine the dramatic scene. Rumours about it immediately reached the camp. The soldiers and the condemned turned to Pouliopoulos. His eyes burned. The lives of 106 hung by a thread. Pouliopoulos' words were their only chance.

There was dead silence after his speech. If one soldier threw down his gun all would do so. The order to fire was given, but nobody raised his gun. They were too overcome. The Fascist at their head took out his pistol and shot Pouliopoulos dead. So a huge tree was felled.

The other comrades of ours, Xipolitos, Makris, Giannakos and Lambropoulos fell dead by his side, and all passed away to eternity.

The Fascist animal in charge ordered the firing squad to leave immediately as if the victims were chasing them. The bodies lay where they had fallen. After 36 hours the peasants of St Stephanos came and buried them in a common grave.

On 6 June, between two and three in the afternoon, the mother of Pouliopoulos was awakened by a nightmare in which a king said to her: 'Do you know what they have done? Do you know where to find your baby?' The mother of Giannakos at the same moment saw an evzone pull a knife out of his belt and thrust it into his chest. In this way the tragedy of Nezero was told to the mothers.

The tragedy of Nezero hung over the camp at Larissa lived until it was closed. On 7 September 1943 Italy signed an armistice, Badoglio took power, and finito Mussolini, the ex-Socialist, while in Italy the workers prepared for power and seized their factories. The Italians at Larissa camp were just happy to go home.

The Germans had no confidence in them, and took over the camp. They started interrogations to discover the Communists who had survived Nezero. They released all those whom they could not prove were Communists. Thus Petsis and Spaneas were released. Simos was kept as a possible Jew. Petsis had to go to Athens and get his papers.

All those from Acronauplia, Stalinists and Trotskyists alike, and including Hadjichristos, H Soulas and G Krokas, were transferred to Haidari. There they suffered another agony which finished with the historic executions of 1 May 1944 at Kaisariani.

Simos stayed with about 60 others. He was kept for work in the interior after the others had been released, until his papers arrived. He was captured on 7 January 1943 and released 11 or 12 months later.

Finishing his story, Simos added in tears that among the clothes from the Red Cross given to the prisoners, he had been given a blanket marked PP. It was indeed the blanket of Pouliopoulos."

The Resistance Movement against Hitler and the KKE

Trotskyists did participate in the Resistance movement against Hitler but due to their small size and the fact that they were working under triple repression: Metaxas dictatorship, after Hitler's Occupation and then the KKE's secret police to openly say the word Trotskyist, whilst on the outside was a sure death sentence. They supported acts against Hitlerism and many did indeed lead guerilla groups, but they were against the theory of 'guerilla war' which the KKE refined - isolated attacks on German occupation forces which led to mass reprisals against the local population.

But what could people do against Hitler's Occupation? Reprisals were inevitable any which way you look at it? Was the KKE wrong to resist Hitler and go to the mountains? Clearly not. What was wrong was the KKE's insistence to link the resistance movement simply to the removal of Hitler's forces - not capitalism in general. In such a manner they were unprepared politically when British forces landed in Greece at the end of WWII. They called them 'liberators' and wrote 'Welcome' all over the walls of Athens and Thessalonika. They disarmed their forces in the name of peace and harmony.

This is where their mistakes became compounded by the fact that Stalin had already agreed to hand Greece over to the western 'sphere of influence' as agreed in Yalta. The KKE had no choice but to follow Stalin's orders. This meant the disarming of the guerillas and the acceptance of Hitler's supporters in the 'new Greece' which actually mirrored the old order. These problems led to the Greek Civil War.

Notes
1.Comrade Stinas had spoken of 'Fascism' both before and after the imposition of the Metaxas dictatorship. Within the ranks of the EOKDE, however, there was a general consensus that the KDEE's analysis of Fascism was derived from their incorrect evaluation of the situation and from other theoretical errors. Our conference described the 4 August dictatorship as a 'military-police regime'.
A relentless ideological struggle against Stinas' tendency occurred in the Acronauplia concentration camp. We exposed their pessimistic evaluation of the correlation of political forces prior to the Metaxas dictatorship and after the Thessalonica events, and also the mechanistic mentality that Stinas brought with him when he split from Stalinism. There was nothing new about Stinas' view of the 'Fascism of 4 August'. He did not accept the analysis of Fascism which Trotsky formulated, he could not throw off his Stalinist past, and, whatever his claims, he never became a Trotskyist. He used the same criteria as the Stalinists to describe the Metaxas dictatorship as Fascist.

Stinas was, nonetheless, careful not to go so far as the Stalinists, and avoided such theories as 'all-out Fascism' and 'Social Fascism', and those of the Archeio-Marxists, through which he himself had lived, first as a supporter of Pouliopoulos in the spring of 1927, and then as a Stalinist that autumn, when he started to persecute the Spartakists and Archeio-Marxists. He also avoided being identified with the later Stalinist ideas, that the choice of the day was between democracy and Fascism, and that one should call for the democratisation of the bourgeois regime.

2. LD Trotsky, *The Death Agony of Capitalism and the Tasks of the Fourth International*, London, 1976, p21.
3. LD Trotsky, 'On the Eve of World War II', *Writings of Leon Trotsky 1939-40*, New York, 1977, p20.
4. LD Trotsky, 'Manifesto of the Fourth International on the Imperialist War and the World Proletarian Revolution', *Writings of Leon Trotsky 1939-40*, New York, 1977, p222.
5. JP Cannon, 'A Statement on the US Entry into World War II', *The Socialist Workers Party in World War II*, New York, 1987, p209.
6. We have learned that Barjotas, a GPU agent, gave orders at a meeting in his headquarters to kill any oppositionist on the spot. During the events of December he was heard to say that he went round like a mad dog, pistol in hand, ready to 'bite' any revolutionaries who came out into the street following Lenin's strategy of turning the imperialist war into a civil war. In the end he gave a record to the GPU of the hundreds of Trotskyists and oppositionists that he had liquidated.

For our part, we faced their jails or interrogations, those inquisitions of frightful tortures, and the executions at the hands of these savages, in order to try to save our people from their hands, or to learn whether they were dead or alive.

We looked for months to discover the fate of our comrades. Sometimes we only found their graves. The brother of Mimis Belias, for example, opened a mass grave by the Vyon stream. There, thanks to things he knew and clothes which had not rotted away, he recognised the decomposed body of his brother Mimis. He lifted it up and held it in his arms so that the rotten flesh and earth stuck to him. He burst into tears and had a breakdown, and afterwards he became chronically depressed. Mimis Belias was arrested by the OPLA on 12 December 1944. His corpse had a broken arm and three gold teeth missing. There were hundreds of such murders, and hundreds of such stories.

Thus these most dishonourable and the most counter-revolutionary atrocities against us came to light. These crimes were a blow against the proletarian revolution.

EAM-ELAS

Loukas Karliaftis': Speech in the Athens Debate between KKE and Trotskyists

A well-intentioned discussion about solving the problems faced by the workers' movement, about the struggles of the proletariat for their social liberation and that of oppressed classes generally, as well as a settlement of the differences which exist amongst the various tendencies in the workers' movement, must presume some definitions and the acceptance of certain principles.

For us, for the KDKE (Fourth International), these principles, both the starting point and the method of investigation, are to be found in the acceptance of the teachings of Marx and Engels and of the other great teachers: Lenin, Luxemburg and Trotsky. It consists first of all of the acceptance of their method, historical materialism, and secondly of the laws which characterise capitalist society and economy, and determine its development and decline. Thirdly, it consists in recognising the class struggle, and accepting that this struggle within class society leads unavoidably to the dictatorship of the proletariat. Here is what Marx himself says about this part of his teachings:

'As to myself, no credit is due to me for discovering either the existence of classes in modern society or the struggle between them. Long before me, bourgeois historians had described the historical development of this class struggle, and bourgeois economists the economic anatomy of the classes. What I did that was new was to demonstrate:
 (1) that the existence of classes is merely linked to particular historical phases in the development of production;

(2) that class struggle necessarily leads to the dictatorship of the proletariat;
(3) that this dictatorship itself only constitutes the transition to the abolition of all classes and to a classless society.'[1]

Lenin, in fighting all the traitors to Marxism and in analysing the above quotation from Marx's letter to Weydemeyer, writes:
'In these words, Marx succeeded in expressing with striking clarity, firstly, the chief and radical difference between his theory and that of the foremost and most profound thinkers of the bourgeoisie; and, secondly, the essence of his theory of the state.
'It is often said and written that the main point in Marx's theory is the class struggle. But this is wrong. And this wrong notion very often results in an opportunist distortion of Marxism and its falsification in a spirit acceptable to the bourgeoisie. For the theory of the class struggle was created not by Marx, but by the bourgeoisie before Marx and, generally speaking, it is acceptable to the bourgeoisie. Those who recognise only the class struggle are not yet Marxists; they may be found to be still within the bounds of bourgeois thinking and bourgeois politics. To confine Marxism to the theory of the class struggle means curtailing Marxism, distorting it, reducing it to something acceptable to the bourgeoisie. Only he is a Marxist who extends the recognition of the class struggle to the recognition of the dictatorship of the proletariat. This is what constitutes the most profound distinction between the Marxist and the ordinary petty (as well as big) bourgeois. This is the touchstone on which the real understanding and recognition of Marxism should be tested.'[2]

Fourthly, it consists of the recognition of the international character of the struggle of the proletariat.

Rosa Luxemburg, in her struggle against Social Democracy, showed that whoever ignores in theory or practice one of these two principles -- the class struggle or the internationalism of the proletarian struggle -- invariably becomes a supporter and defender of reactionary capitalist regimes, and turns into an agent of the bourgeoisie inside the proletariat, to use Lenin's phrase. All the modern history of the proletarian struggle from the epoch of Social Democracy until today is nothing more than a positive or a negative confirmation of this view, which was supported by the consistent pupils of Marx and Engels against every type of revisionist in every epoch.

If anyone asks the leaders of the KKE, they will declare the teachings of Marx, Engels and Lenin to be correct. They will say that they 'accept' as correct the teachings of Marx on the capitalist regime and the class struggle under which it, unavoidably according to Marx, leads to the dictatorship of the proletariat. They even 'accept' the teachings of Lenin on capitalism and its last imperialist stage. They 'accept' the teachings of Lenin (which is but an extension and concretisation of Marx) on imperialist wars and the tasks they pose for the revolutionary vanguard and the working class.

For us, consistent pupils of Marx, Engels and Lenin, there is no need for a new theoretical reaffirmation of their teachings. Our work is inseparable from and scientifically based upon our great teachers. Practically the whole of current history is a great confirmation, positive or negative, of their teachings. The Paris Commune and the victorious October Revolution are their positive confirmations. The latter is the greatest victory for the proletariat, which was made possible by the correct application of these teachings. On the other hand, the Chinese Revolution of 1925-27, the German and Spanish Revolutions and the Second World War are defeats which occurred because of leaders who in practice had negated these teachings.

If we are to be serious, for a sincere debater for the KKE, for world Stalinism, for a debater who respects science, the task is to prove theoretically and in practice why this theory, with its basic premises and its conclusions, does not correspond to our epoch, and why we are faced with the necessity of revising it. A general declaration of changed circumstances is at best a weakness and a subterfuge. At worst, it is conscious deceit and a betrayal of the titanic struggle which the proletariat is waging. The KKE does not lack material means. On the contrary, no other tendency has ever had so many resources at its disposal as does the Stalinist current. For more than 20 years we have waited for this opportunity but in vain. Scientific discussion has been replaced by perfidy, falsity, lies, deceit, sycophancy and physical violence. But these methods have not relieved the KKE of its obligations, it has increased them.

The current political situation can be analysed by a Marxist only from the point of view of its historical connections and development. Every natural or social phenomenon has its history, and only during the process of historical development is it possible for them to be understood clearly and completely. All modern science is a confirmation of this basic view of Marxist teaching. Today was born of yesterday. Tomorrow is determined by the dynamic of today. Only in the light of this investigation is it possible to reveal the correctness or incorrectness of the politics of the different tendencies inside the workers' movement and to prove their social nature.

War is the most important feature of our epoch. The war of 1939-45 was an imperialist, reactionary conflict between the rich and the 'hungry' imperialist powers. The involvement of the Soviet Union in this war was unavoidable, and was determined by the international nature of the world economy. The war waged by the Soviet Union was defensive and progressive, and the international working class had the duty to defend it. But the progressive nature of the war on the part of the Soviet Union (the defence of nationalised ownership) transformed neither the general imperialist character of the war nor the content and obligations of the proletarian struggle for social revolution. The war made nonsense of all the Stalinist 'theories' of the peaceful coexistence of the Soviet Union with capitalism and of 'Socialism in one country'.

All the theoretical work of Lenin and the Communist International and the policies they developed in the first four congresses maintained their importance for the second imperialist war and will continue to maintain it for all the wars which will be waged by imperialism if the proletariat allows it. The existence of the Soviet Union does not change the nature of imperialism. The Soviet Union was thought of by its founders as none other than an advanced outpost of the world workers' front. This is the teaching of Lenin. All those who deny this revise Marxism-Leninism and break the internationalism of the proletarian struggle with disastrous consequences.

War and revolution are the most important events in human history. The Marxist left wing of Social Democracy -- Lenin, Trotsky and Luxemburg -- broke off all relations with the Second International precisely on this issue.

The question of war is very important, and it must be given its proper place in any serious discussion amongst the tendencies inside the workers' movement. Our party proposed this topic for the first of these three discussions. The outbreak of the second imperialist war was impossible without the defeat of the proletariat. This defeat was not possible but for the abandonment and revision of Marxist teachings by its own leadership. Just as the outbreak of the First World War confirmed the opportunist and treacherous nature of the leadership of the Second International, so the outbreak of the Second World War confirmed the petty-bourgeois degeneration of and the betrayals carried out by the leadership of the Communist International. If the outbreak of war presupposes an absolute weakening of the revolutionary strength of the working class, then the war itself, with its horrors and destruction, forces the working class into the forefront of history, and increases immeasurably its social dynamism and revolutionary strength.

This phenomenon showed itself quite markedly and clearly in Greece. Let us look at the main changes which the war brought about in the Greek economy and in the regrouping of social forces. It dislocated the capitalist economy of the country. The theft of national wealth, of the products of the country by the imperialist occupation in cooperation with the domestic plutocracy, created intolerable conditions of life for the oppressed masses. With inflation it wiped out any savings of the petty-bourgeois layers in town and country, and impelled them to take a decisive turn to the left. The bankruptcy of the bourgeois parties was complete, whilst in the working masses, a passion for a decisive social transformation was brewing. The turn of the masses to the left brought the old revolutionary party of the proletariat, the KKE, into the leadership of their struggle, due to the enormous prestige of the October Revolution which they saw this party as representing.

These developments in the consciousness of the masses led capitalist reaction in the country to make a desperate attempt to maintain its social rule and enter an alliance with both imperialisms -- the Allied and the Axis. In the face of revolution, the imperialists are united. This action of theirs led the country into a situation of civil war, and in consequence all but wiped out the power of the capitalist state.

The situation in our country at the end of the civil was definitely revolutionary. But what were the politics of the KKE if not a complete negation of Marxist-Leninist teaching?

In place of the class and of class struggle -- the nation and nationalist struggle.

In place of the class struggle -- the collaboration of classes and class unity: in other words the subordination of the proletariat and the oppressed masses to the bourgeoisie.

In place of declarations to cultivate international proletarian solidarity -- the cultivation of nationalist hatred and nationalist patriotic sentiments.

In place of the struggle against the imperialists -- subjugation to Anglo-Saxon imperialism. Hundreds are the victims, militants who died because they opposed the excessive Anglo-friendliness of the KKE leadership, and carried out anti-British and anti-imperialist propaganda. Look at the relevant decisions of the Eleventh Plenum of the Central Committee of the KKE.

In place of the Socialist revolution -- the historically defunct 'Popular Democracy' with its respect for private property.

All of these things are known -- as are Lebanon, Caserta and the National Unity government.

The leadership of the KKE held power in Greece and handed it over to the Greek capitalists and their partners and patrons in Britain.

There was no problem of power for the KKE and the EAM. The opportunity existed to consolidate and maintain power. We ask: why didn't the KKE struggle to remain in power and implement its 'Popular Democratic Programme'? Why did it bring British imperialism to Greece?

What is the nature of the 'Popular Frontist' policy which its ministers carried out when in Papandreou's government? Was it bourgeois or not? Did it serve capitalist interests or not? Was the stabilisation of the currency carried out against the interests of the oppressed masses or not? Is it true that Porfirogenis[3] was the one who introduced Law 118 concerning the 'surplus of workers' in capitalist businesses? And we ask: if all these things are correct, how can we characterise the politics of the KKE?

And December? We must speak out clearly. December was not a revolution organised by the leaders of the EAM but a counter-revolution, an attack by Anglo-Saxon reaction against which the oppressed masses, and especially the proletariat of Athens and the Piraeus, defended themselves heroically.

December was systematically prepared using every possible method: the security forces, civil war, Lebanon and Caserta, with Ralis and Papandreou, with Scobie and Spiliotopoulus, with the court tribunals in the Middle East and Surmata and by Anglo-Greek imperialism.

Why did the EAM's leaders refuse to form a revolutionary government when 90 percent of the population was under their influence and the whole country under their control? Why did it not declare that no unity could exist with the exploiters and murderers, in other words, with the capitalist class, but instead fought for a 'New National

Government'? With whom? Why did it not call on the natural allies of the Greek oppressed, the world proletariat, to aid it in its struggle? Why did the Stalinist government of the Soviet Union say not a single word of sympathy for the heroic struggle of the Greek masses during the December events?

The Greek proletariat and the other oppressed masses were defeated in December because their defeat was prepared before December and during December.

In December, the endless heroism and courage of the revolutionary proletariat confronted a malicious, crafty, cunning, criminal and historically bankrupt class: world capitalist reaction. This class -- dark and criminal -- appears strong with its international bonds and its solidarity when it confronts its enemy: the revolutionary proletarian class. The proletariat -- militant and heroic and with endless resources of bravery and sacrifice appeared with its international links and its internationalist solidarity broken. Its leadership, however, did not direct it towards a realisation of its historic mission, but placed it under... a 'New National Government'.

For this purpose, it appealed to the great imperialist 'Democracy of the Atlantic'. The 'leadership' of the Greek proletariat asked for help from Roosevelt, not from the world proletariat. Without a doubt, the Stalinist leadership had -- essentially from 1934 and definitively from 1943 -- broken the internationalist links of the proletariat with the dissolution of the Communist International.

Lebanon, Caserta and, in December, Varkiza determined the political line and the social nature of the EAM's leadership, proving it to be petty-bourgeois, objectively placed within the framework of the capitalist regime serving the bourgeoisie.

If Anglo-Greek capitalist reaction moved towards December, this was not due to fear of or in reaction to the politics pursued by the EAM leadership, but to the direct threat posed by the armed and deeply anti-capitalist disposition of the masses. The question of disarming the masses was, for Anglo-Greek and world capitalist reaction, a question of life and death.

With its victory in December, Greek capitalist reaction, based on the tanks and guns of Scobie, re-established its political rule. Its immediate aim was the re-establishment of its oppressive state machine and the stabilisation of its rule. United and decisive in carrying this out, it was aided and directed by its patron, British imperialism.

With the disarming of the masses (and the amnesty of the EAM's leaders at Varkiza) the main problem which emerged for the Greek capitalists was and continues to be the 'rebuilding' of the economy, for which the oppressed masses have to pay. For this task, the disarming of the masses was insufficient, their spirit had to be broken. Directly or indirectly, their organisations had to be dissolved. The workers had to be broken into isolated and subjugated individuals. This task was undertaken by the various neo-Fascist organisations and gangs. At the same time, an economic offensive was unleashed on behalf of the capitalist oligarchy with the weapon of inflation.

Workers' and employees' wages were repeatedly wiped out. All the stabilisations of the drachma which took place had as their aim a continuing cut in living standards. And the attack on living standards is continuing with the high prices announced for goods, and the implementation of indirect taxes.

All of this comes at a time when the capitalist government is giving endless grants to bankers, industrialists and traders in the form of loans, which inflation wipes out at one tenth of the initial cost.

While the economic attack is continuing, alongside it is an attempt to 'legalise' the dictatorial government which is concealed by a parliamentary façade for external consumption and for the deception of the world proletariat. World capitalist reaction, from Churchill's Tories to the pseudo-Socialist lackeys of imperialism, the Labour Party, in England, from the 'Democratic' bankers of New York and Washington to the 'Popular Democrats' of France, is struggling with deceit and armed force to crush the insurrections of capital's slaves. And while their cannons, tanks and aeroplanes bombard the slaves of Indonesia, Indochina, India, China and elsewhere, they send their 'observers' to Greece to bring the king back to the throne 'with due regard for the law'.

Greek capitalist reaction, with the support of world capitalism, and completely conscious of its class interests, is advancing towards the realisation of its aims of stabilising its power and its exploitative regime.

What are the policies of today's leadership of the working class? 'Peaceful democratic development', in other words the negation of the struggle to achieve the historic aims of the proletariat, the struggle for Socialism. The leadership of the KKE throughout this period has objectively aided domestic and foreign reaction to achieve its aims. It aided them with its politics, which condemned the working class to inactivity and passivity, or dissipated and squandered the willingness of the masses to struggle, with its slogans and cries of 'Don't! You will provoke a monarchist coup!', with its denunciation of all those militants who would not disarm at Varkiza -- in other words those who would not stand with their arms folded and wait to be slaughtered by the Fascists, and with non-participation in the elections, with the utopia of a 'Pan-democratic Front'.

Instead of supporting the struggle of the working class in the organisations of the working class on a world scale (according to the teachings of Marx, Engels and Lenin, and according to the global experience of the workers' movement), it supported attempts at making a deal with bourgeois politicians of the 'centre' and the 'left', Sofoulis, Kafandaris and Sofianopoulos, as if it was not they who, with every demagogic utterance, were not attacking the mass movement. As if it was not the government of the 'Democratic Centre' which had staged an electoral coup in March!

Comrades, are these coincidental mistakes, or even just a mistaken political line? No. There is a complete consistency in the political line of the KKE. The politics of the KKE are determined by a complete denial of the proletarian revolution in Greece, from the abandonment of the old revolutionary programme to the acceptance of the possibility of bourgeois democracy in the epoch of imperialism. We are dealing with politics which are determined by the acceptance of a regime of private ownership. Here, comrades, a basic opposition exists to the revolutionary politics of Marx and Lenin and to the Fourth International which continues to this day.

The plans of domestic and foreign reaction do not stop at ensuring and maintaining their political and economic domination. The anarchy of production impels capitalism to a constant quest for profit and raw materials. This leads unavoidably to imperialist war. Instead of solving the contradictions of capitalism, war intensifies them, impoverishing the masses and forcing capitalism sooner or later into new wars. The historical dilemma of the epoch, 'Socialism or Barbarism' is placed decisively in front of humanity.

World capitalism today is emerging from another war. Despite great destruction of the means of production in countries like Germany and Japan, it does so with its productive capacities increased. But the standard of living for the masses fell drastically during the war. Their purchasing power was lowered to half its pre-war level. Capitalism needs new markets for selling its goods. The Soviet Union controls and rules over a significant portion of our planet. And from the point of view of the social nature of the regime, it is an enemy of capitalism.

World capitalism, under the leadership of American imperialism, is preparing an anti-Soviet war. But an outbreak of war is impossible without the previous defeat of the working class. This is what world capitalism is preparing to do. From a strategic point of view, the geographical situation of Greece will give it an important role in any such anti-Soviet war -- if the proletariat does not stop it with a social revolution. One of the aims of domestic and world reaction is to turn Greece into an anti-Soviet and anti-working class bridgehead.

From the analysis we have made, we have demonstrated that the interests of Greek and British capitalism, although not identical, generally coincide. Greek capitalism bases its hopes of rebuilding its economy on the support of Anglo-Saxon imperialism. Both domestic and foreign capitalist reaction feel undying hatred for the movement of the masses for their social liberation. They both nurture the same hatred for the Soviet Union.

British imperialism has to defend its interests in the Middle East. The route to India lies through the eastern Mediterranean. The struggle for oil occurs today mainly in the Middle East. These factors force British imperialism to take a particular interest in Greece and Turkey.

These are the aims of imperialism, both domestic and foreign -- the stabilisation of capitalist power wherever it has been shaken, the rebuilding of the capitalist economy on the backs of the working masses, the crushing of the mass movement, and assured strategic bases for the anti-Soviet war. The Greek proletariat and the oppressed masses must react and struggle to frustrate the plans of imperialism.

The struggle against Greek capitalism is a struggle against world imperialism, and, conversely, the struggle against world capitalism is not possible without a parallel struggle against Greek capitalist reaction.

The fronts are clearly distinguishable for all those who want to see -- world capitalist reaction on the one side and the world working class on the other. This is the only way to pose the problem and the only way it can be tackled correctly and successfully.

The KKE puts the question of the removal of the British foremost, and whatever the oppressed masses may do is derived from this. The removal of the British is not seen as the outcome of the activity of the masses, but as a problem of good will and Allied diplomacy in which bourgeois 'patriots' are to be sought. Since these tasks must precede any other forms of struggle, they serve only to postpone the mass struggle.

Our party, as an internationalist party, confronts the problem from an internationalist point of view. Our party has never stopped carrying out the most decisive and irreconcilable struggle against imperialism. In this struggle, it has suffered many losses, among them our best cadres. The expulsion of the British from Greece, and from all the countries they are occupying, is seen as the result of the activity of the masses and chiefly the British working class. Our allies in the struggle to foil the plans of British imperialism will not be found amongst bourgeois politicians, but amongst the British and the world proletariat. We must make a firm distinction between British imperialism and the working masses of Britain. The first is an ally of local domestic capitalist reaction. Every struggle against Greek capitalism is also a struggle against British imperialism. In our struggle for our economic demands, for our trade union and political rights, we must seek and obtain aid from the British proletariat. British soldiers stationed here should side with us. The same British soldiers should ask to return to their homes.

At every opportunity we should seek to fraternise with British troops -- just as we should demand fraternisation with the Greek soldiers who are being sent to attack the struggles of our brothers. The arms they are carrying can and must be used against our common class enemy. The British working class must rise up and halt the plans of British imperialism.

Class against class, the old Leninist slogan which paralysed imperialist reaction in the epoch of Red October, must be heard everywhere. It can give us victory and it will -- because the working class is all-powerful. It is simply unaware of its strength because every type of confidence trickster confuses its thinking. The historical rôle of the revolutionary vanguard is to dispel confusion and show the path.

The Greek working class has suffered countless significant defeats. But none of these were decisive. That is why the movement intensified on an international scale. The spirit of the masses persists, although not as intensely as before. We have both explained the causes of the defeats and named their architects. Today the economic situation of the working class is dreadful. Inflation is rising. Starvation wages are already losing their value. The working class will enter into struggle in order to defend its livelihood.

The organisation of these struggles is the direct and immediate responsibility of the revolutionary vanguard.

In the countryside a number of factors have influenced and determined the development of a significant peasant movement which grew large during the war and the occupation. These are:

a) The small landholder using primitive methods of cultivation and the small peasant as well, thus only produce small profits per annum.

b) There is a large variation in prices between agricultural and industrial goods, due to the monopolistic form of industrial capital, which acts against agricultural produce. This results in the absorbing of a section of agricultural capital by industrial capital.

c) Agricultural produce is mainly of produce (raisins, olives, figs, etc) for foreign markets. They are distributed by various capitalist concerns or by traders who also take a significant cut from the income.

d) Taxes. The capitalist class, in order to preserve its exploitative regime, is obliged to maintain a hypertrophic state mechanism. In 1939 this consumed more than half the national income. A significant part of the budget for this weighs down on the peasantry in the form of direct taxation.

These factors, combined with the destruction of war and occupation, created a revolutionary peasant movement and ensured that the position of the poor peasant masses was alongside that of the urban proletariat for the realisation of Socialism.

This is the movement which Greek reaction attempted to annihilate. Unleashing a civil war in the countryside, ELAS guerrillas and other poor peasants rushed into the mountains to defend their lives and the lives of the fellow citizens.

This movement took a most lively form in Thessaly and Macedonia, where the peasant masses were more educated and adopted a class position. But there is another important factor, that of national minorities. The attitude of Greek capitalism was always oppressive to the minorities. After the war, their attitude was criminal. Seeking to realise the imperialist plans in the Balkans, they attempted to eliminate the national minorities.

The new guerrilla movement, which is the defence of the poor peasants, both Greek and foreign-speaking, against the attacks of the capitalist reaction which is trying to put its exploitative and imperialist schemes into practice, became a significant development in Thessaly and Macedonia. All the 'exterminating missions' achieved only one thing -- they strengthened the movement. But the activity of the guerrillas could not, on its own, crush the capitalist attack. Left on its own and based on its own resources, the new guerrilla movement will sooner or later be forced to submit. The working class of the cities and other oppressed layers must defend the struggle of the poor peasants and the national minorities. They can defend it by organising their own struggles for their economic demands, and frustrating the aims of capitalist reaction. Part of their demands should relate to the slogan for ending the terrorism in the countryside and for a general amnesty for the fighters of the poor peasantry.

Under these conditions, the tasks of the revolutionary vanguard are clearly defined -- the abandonment of any utopian idea of 'stable democratic development', which cannot be achieved even with the help of a section of the bourgeoisie, its 'progressive democratic wing'. Such a grouping does not exist within the bourgeois class in the epoch of its decline. The period of democracy has passed. Bourgeois society is facing a period of decline. Today the ruling class must resort to Fascist methods of rule to maintain its regime. Only the Socialist Soviet Democracy can take humanity out of the chaos and barbarism into which capitalism is leading us. Whoever denies this view today becomes, whether they want to or not, a supporter of capitalism. The Socialist Revolution! That must be the main strategic aim of the working class.

But at this juncture in Greece we are about to face the attacks of capitalist reaction. And we can be successful with the immediate organisation of the struggles of the masses. Much time has been lost, and reaction has been winning. Our party declares that its main goal is the unity of the working class and other oppressed layers in a class front to fight for work -- for wage rises index-linked to inflation, and for trade union and political freedom. On the basis of this minimum programme we call on all workers and all the oppressed to organise themselves and to defend their struggle on a national level. Workers' democracy must be honoured by all.

But if this minimum programme is enough to unite the oppressed in a United Front of struggle, it is not enough in itself for a United Front of the working class. We call on all the workers' parties -- the KKE, the SK-ELD, the AKE -- to form a United Front on the basis of the following minimum programme:

1) The organisation of struggles for the economic demands of workers, of employees and of the peasant masses;
2) For trade union and political freedom;
3) For an amnesty for popular militants;
4) For the organisation of workers' guards;
5) For the dissolution of the pseudo-parliament and for the declaration of elections to a Constituent Assembly;
6) For the ousting of the British by the methods of internationalist struggle; expose the imperialist aims of Anglo-Saxon capitalism and exposing the reactionary anti-working class rôle of British policy in Greece; show the distinction between the British proletariat and British capitalism; distribute fraternising propaganda in the British camps;[4] appeal to the class solidarity of the British and world proletariat through workers' organisations; oppose every armed intervention against the workers' movement but without stopping our struggle to fraternise with the armed soldiers; for decisiveness, for commitment to and for the honouring of worker's democracy.

On the basis of this minimum programme we call in every trade union, in every factory, in every community, in every city and village, for the democratic and proportional election of committees of the workers' alliance, which will organise and lead the workers' struggles.

Every party will maintain its independence, its right to propagate its full programme and its right openly to criticise.

Loukas Karliaftis
Notes
1. Karl Marx, Letter to Joseph Weydemeyer, 5 March 1852, K Marx and F Engels, *Selected Correspondence*, Moscow, 1975, p64.
2. VI Lenin, 'State and Revolution', *Collected Works*, Volume 25, Moscow, 1977, p416.
3. One of the Communist Party's ministers in Papandreou's government.
4. An attempt was made to establish contact between British revolutionaries in uniform and the Greek movement, in spite of language difficulties. John Giles Henderson was able to make four contacts with members of the Greek Trotskyist movement who worked in the army stores in the Piraeus. Although hampered by a lack of knowledge of the language, he was able to acquaint them with the positions of the rest of the Trotskyist movement by passing to them copies of the Revolutionary Communist Party's journals, the *Workers International News* and *Socialist Appeal*, and those of the US Socialist Workers Party, *The Militant* and *Fourth International*. Trotskyists in the British army in Egypt took considerable

risks to leaflet the troops there calling on them to refuse to fire on their Greek working class brothers (Alex Acheson, 'The Wartime Agitation of a Trotskyist Soldier', appendix 2 of Sam Bornstein and Al Richardson, *War and the International*, London, 1986, p247).

Elas-Greek Partisan on the March

Bibliography

L Karliaftis , History of the Bolshevism in Greece
A.Georgiadou & Katsoulakis, First Congress of the SEKE(K)
KKE, Five years of Struggle 1931-36
KKE, Short History of the KKE by the CC (Oct '88)
Kordatos, Capitalism, Reminisces, History of Greek Labour Movement
Leonarditis, Greek Socialist Movement During WWI
Stinas, Reminisces: 50 Years under the Flag of the Socialist Revolution
George B Leon, Greece nad the Great Powers 1914-17
D George Kousoulas, Revolution and Defeat: The Story of the Greek Communist Party
Stavrianos, The Balkans
L. Trotsky, Collected Writings 1930-34, History of the Russian Revolution, The Left Opposition 3 Volumes, New Courses, The Revolution Betrayed, Third International after Lenin
Averroff-Tossizza, By Fire and Axe

ABBREVIATIONS

CI= communist international
CP= communist party
EGSEE= Short lived stalinist United Confederation of Greek Workers
GSEE= General Confederation of Greek Workerss
ILO= International Left Opposition

FOOTNOTES

1 Kordatos Kapitalismos p.50 Edition 1982
2 George Leon GREECE & THE Great Powers
Edition 1974
3 Sintomi Istoria tou KKE
4 Collected Works Volume 23
5 Thesis Sosialistikou Kommatos 1917
6 Leontaritis, To Elliniko Sosialistiko Kinima kata
tin Diarkia tou Protou Pagkosmiou Polemou
7 The Story of the Greek Communist Party
8 Rizospastis
9 Proto Sinedrio tou SEKE
10 Anamnises-Stinas
11 Revolution and Defeat-Kousoulas
12 Ibid
13 Rizospastis
14 National Library
15 Kommunistiki Enosis
16 Rizospastis
17 Third International after Lenin
18 Rizospastis
19 First Declaration of KKE
20 Revolution and Defeat
21 Rizospastis
22 An Explanation Concerning Kondilis Elections

www.ingramcontent.com/pod-product-compliance
Lightning Source LLC
Chambersburg PA
CBHW060257290526
45789CB00001B/342